When Retail
Customers Count

When Retail Customers Count

How understanding customer traffic patterns can help good retailers become great retailers

Mark Ryski

authorHOUSE

1663 LIBERTY DRIVE, SUITE 200
BLOOMINGTON, INDIANA 47403
(800) 839-8640
www.authorhouse.com

LIBRARY OF CONGRESS CATALOGING-IN-PUBLICATION DATA: 2005900102
Ryski, Mark.
    When Retail Customers Count: How understanding customer traffic patterns can help good
retailers become great retailers / Mark Ryski.
    p. cm.
Includes Index
ISBN: 1-4208-2475-9 (sc)
ISBN: 1-4208-2476-7 (dj)
1. Retailing.   2. Marketing.   3. Sales   4. Business Management I. Title

First published by AuthorHouse 01/05/05

To the people who count the most to me—Corine, Taylor and Cole

Table of Contents

	Acknowledgments	ix
	Foreword	xi
Introduction	Why Count Customers?	1
Chapter 1	Measuring the Impact of Advertising & Promotions	7
Chapter 2	Setting and Refining Store Hours	45
Chapter 3	The Impact of Weather on Traffic	67
Chapter 4	Sales Conversion	85
Chapter 5	Staff Planning	121
Chapter 6	Special Events and Holidays	155
Chapter 7	Multi-location Traffic Analysis	177
Chapter 8	Web, Phone and Store Traffic	215
Chapter 9	The Strategic Value of Traffic Insights	241
Chapter 10	Traffic and Service Businesses	267
Conclusion	Why Count Customers?	279
	About the Author	283
	Permissions	285
	Index	289

Acknowledgments

WRITING A BOOK IS HARD. Now I know just how hard. In order to get the job done, you need a passion for the topic, an appetite for labor, and most importantly, other people to help you "write" the book. There are many dedicated people who were involved in *When Retail Customers Count*, some directly and others indirectly.

First, Donald Anderson, my business partner, writing coach and right arm. As a tireless fighter and supporter of the traffic counting cause, he was instrumental to this project in every way. I am also deeply indebted to the HeadCount Corporation team, especially Richard Sefcik and Kirsten Boyd, who worked tirelessly reviewing copy and refining graphs and charts. To Andrew Gilchrist and Thomas MacArthur, for without their engineering genius we wouldn't have the ability to collect and analyze traffic data.

To Sean Harrison, CL Couldwell and Danyon Reeves at swur.com corporation for bringing clarity to the graphics and charts that help tell the traffic story words alone could not. To Howard Poon, creative director extraordinaire, for his work on the book cover. And, of course, to Peter Miller, Jenn Robison and Cheryl Eger at AuthorHouse.

To Gordon Meeberg and Howard Hunchak for their comments, questions and suggestions that have undoubtedly made this book better. And to Garry Schultz for his sage advice in the early days when it was most needed.

To Paul McElhone and the Canadian Institute of Retailing and Services at the University of Alberta for being supportive and providing a platform from which we are able to preach the gospel of traffic analysis.

To the many great retail executives, managers, and store-level personnel I have had the opportunity to work with, who have embraced all that traffic analysis can do.

And, lastly, to two people who have most greatly influenced the way I look at business problems and try to solve them, Darren Pentelechuk and Bruce Johnson.

Foreword

WITH THE ADVENT OF the "Big Box" retailers, shrinking margins, and dwindling returns, small, mid-size, and major retailers alike are looking for meaningful ways to fine-tune their businesses. Mark Ryski has put together a tool box packed-full with practical and helpful ways to show retailers how to be more strategic in the retail game. The well-crafted and well-written chapters of *When Retail Customers Count* begin with theory that for many of us seems at first to be rooted in common sense but Mark cleverly peels away layer after layer of interpretation to deepen and broaden our insights into why it is not only important to count traffic but it is essential to take these findings and properly analyze them on a continual basis. No one will put this book down without learning a great deal. And if any of you feel frustrated with the results you're getting with your business or feel that the only solutions available are to continue running your business the way you always have, then Mark Ryski's book is a "must read." His years of experience bring a refreshing approach to the way retailers need to view their most prized possession... *the customer.*

After many years of managing a specialty retail operation, I can tell you that many decisions that I made about advertising, staffing, and performance optimization often came from the gut because, as managers and owner/managers, we were expected to have, and believed we did have, the best feel for the pulse of our businesses. Today, this is not enough. Today's managers and owners need to develop the "science" of retail. And any time you can bring science and intuition together you end up with a strategic position that ensures profitability. It's all about taking your companies to a more professional management style. Mark's book will give you an instrument to better analyze the effectiveness of many of your day-to-day, season-to-season, and year-to-year decisions.

Many of you might ask "Why should I start looking at traffic counts? I can't keep up with all the other responsibilities I have." Why? Because the gems you take away from analytically looking at traffic counts will directly impact your bottom line. Why? Because as retailers, you must always strive to become the brightest and the best merchants in your industry. Why? Because the retailers who use the information from interpreting traffic counts for analyzing conversion rates, for tracking multi-location traffic, for developing effective advertising campaigns, and for optimizing staff planning will have a competitive edge. Can you afford not to read this book? A pretty rhetorical question, I'd say.

Not very often is there a meaningful retail book that isn't just for the "big guys." Mark has managed to create a template that can be customized for all retailers regardless of size, product, or service. His professional, relaxed writing style is engaging. He has attacked head-on many of the challenges facing retailers and those in the service sectors. This is a great read full of excellent insights. Whether you are new to the retail game or a seasoned veteran *When Retail Customers Count* is a great reference book for anyone involved in the retail decision-making process. Enjoy!

– Paul McElhone, Executive Director
Canadian Institute of Retailing and Services

Introduction
Why Count Customers?

The most fundamental of retail metrics is largely unused or misused—if you're not looking at traffic information, how are you managing your store?

EARLY IN MY RETAIL CAREER, I spent a lot of time learning. Learning about how retail business—successful retail business—is conducted. I learned about inventory management and about recruiting and training staff; I learned about retail selling, customer service, merchandising, and of course, retail marketing. During these years, I watched retail change. I watched the downfall of the traditional department store, the rise of specialty retailing and the advent of the "big box" category killers. I was there when the Internet was going to change the face of retailing forever (it did, but not in the ways pundits were predicting). So here we are.

Retail is undoubtedly a far more complicated and sophisticated business than ever before. Successful retailers need to stay on their toes. History is littered with retail giants once thought to be everlasting fixtures in the retailing landscape, but now gone. However, as much as things have changed, certain fundamentals have remained unchanged—such as prospects needing to visit the store in order to make a purchase. This idea of prospect "traffic" is one of the few constants in an otherwise constantly changing retail landscape. Furthermore, it is a notion that applies to virtually every retailer. So why doesn't everybody track traffic? Good question.

I didn't start out being a retail traffic "guru." Nope. I was just a retail marketing manager for a single location specialty store who was simply trying to understand if his advertising was working or not. Pretty simple question, isn't it? It seemed simple enough when the owner of the store I worked for asked me how we would know if the annual marketing plan I prepared would work—how would we know if this was the right plan? As I hunted for information on measuring retail advertising, I discovered there were no simple answers—there was a lot of general information about marketing effectiveness but none that seemed to be specific enough; none that could help me answer my question.

Ultimately, my quest to find the answer to this question led me to traffic counting.

Not only did monitoring traffic help us understand if our advertising was working or not, it became apparent that traffic information was also very useful in scheduling staff, understanding sales performance, determining store hours, planning in-store events and much, much more. Wow! This traffic information is great stuff. Why couldn't I find anything about traffic counting in all those retail management books I read? Why is that even today, the vast majority of retailers don't even bother to monitor store traffic, and even the ones that do only review the data periodically and usually not in any depth? I don't really have a good answer for this. In fact, to this day, when I talk to retailers (successful major retail chains at that), I often feel like Christopher Columbus trying to convince the magistrates of the fifteenth century that the world is indeed round, not flat.

When Retail Customers Count is the book I would have greatly appreciated reading back in my early days. The book covers a wide range of ways traffic analysis can be used to help retailers (and service businesses that receive pedestrian traffic) manage their operations more effectively. The book is as relevant for independent single location retail merchants as it is for executives of mega-chains, and it really doesn't matter if your store sells shoes, shovels, crafts or cars—retailers in virtually every retail segment can benefit from traffic analysis.

Although there is a multitude of uses for traffic analysis, I've focused on the areas that would be of most interest to most retailers. Specifically, here's what is in store (pardon the pun):

- **Chapter 1: Measuring the Impact of Advertising and Promotions**

  It's true, you really can measure the impact of your advertising and promotions. This chapter is full of examples of advertising traffic responses, setting objectives and the like.

- **Chapter 2: Setting and Refining Store Hours**

  Traffic analysis can provide all sorts of insights to assist with decision support, and setting store hours is one of those questions that retailers are constantly grappling with. Traffic analysis can help.

- **Chapter 3: The Impact of Weather on Traffic**

  You can't control the weather, but you can control what you do when weather happens. This chapter will describe the different ways that weather can impact traffic and what you can do to make the most of it.

- **Chapter 4: Sales Conversion—Turning Shoppers into Buyers**

  This is arguably the most critical chapter in the book, as sales conversion is among the most important performance measures in retail. This chapter is a must read.

- **Chapter 5: Staff Planning**

  With labor as one of the largest expenses retailers have, using traffic analysis to optimize staff schedules is the best way to make sure you have the right number of staff—not too many and not too few.

- **Chapter 6: Special Events and Holidays**

  Holidays and special events alter traffic patterns in your store, and traffic analysis will show you how you can make the most out of these times.

- **Chapter 7: Multi-location Traffic Analysis**

  Managing multiple locations is a significant challenge, as is doing the traffic analysis for multiple locations. However, the rewards are also significant. Which is your best performing location? Are you sure? Traffic analysis can tell you.

- **Chapter 8: Web, Phone and Store Traffic—The Complete Picture**

  We know, we know—retailing today is more than just "bricks and mortar" physical locations. In this chapter, you will learn how you can (and should) look across all your channels to get a complete view of traffic—in the store, on the Web and by phone.

- **Chapter 9: The Strategic Value of Traffic Insights**

  Traffic analysis is not just for the floor manager or to give the advertising manager a clue about advertising effectiveness; the senior "big brains" of the retail operation can also benefit from traffic analysis. This chapter will show you how.

- **Chapter 10: Traffic and Service Businesses**

  OK, the book title is a bit misleading… The fact is if you run a business that receives customers or prospects into your physical site, you can benefit from traffic analysis. Traffic counting isn't just for retailers.

This is not an academic text nor a step-by-step "how-to" book, but rather a practical guide incorporating real-world examples of how traffic analysis can be used to help you be a more effective retailer—providing specific and detailed examples of how you can manage costs, measure results, and drive performance using traffic analysis.

We use a lot of traffic charts in this book—charts are great. Charts show you in an instant what it would take me many pages to describe. It makes this book richer and (I hope) more meaningful to you, the reader.

If you are a career retailer, what we share in this book will change the way you look at your business. If you're just starting your retail career like I was, we hope this information helps you get farther, faster.

CHAPTER

Measuring the Impact of Advertising & Promotions

How can you tell if your advertising and promotions are working? Start with the right objective!

Measuring the Impact of Advertising and Promotions

ALMOST WITHOUT FAIL, retailers measure the effectiveness of their advertising and promotions by looking in the till. If sales targets were achieved or exceeded expectations after the campaign, then the promotion worked; if sales were lower than expected, then the promotion did not work—it's as simple as that. Or is it?

ADVERTISING EFFECTIVENESS

• Myths about ad effectiveness

• Advertising objectives

• Traffic response ads

• Marketing considerations

• Traffic patterns and ads

• Media mix and traffic

As a retail marketing manager, I was perplexed by what I felt the results of a promotion were as compared to the sales result. For example, we ran a major advertising campaign and I could tell (and so could everyone else) that the store was very busy—clearly the promotion was working—look at the store! But at the end of the promotion, we were disappointed with the sales result. Sales were just "OK." After seeing this pattern over and over, it occurred to me that sales were not the right measure for determining the effectiveness of our advertising.

If you ask any retailer why they advertise, they will usually tell you they do it to drive sales. The problem with this thinking is that, in destination retail, advertising cannot drive sales. In destination retail, the only thing that advertising can do is attract potential customers into your store. Period. After that, there are numerous other factors that will influence whether or not customers actually buy something. In this chapter we will show you how traffic analysis can help you finally answer the question you have been trying to answer for years: does my advertising work?

Myths about measuring advertising

There are two common myths about retail advertising:

1. that it is impossible to accurately measure the impact of advertising, and

2. sales results are the best measure of advertising effectiveness.

Myth number one is simply a cop-out. Though many managers do think about measuring results, many struggle with how to actually do it. It's far easier to just "do what we've always done" and see where the chips fall. It's not that they are all bad managers. The whole idea of measuring the impact of advertising has plagued marketers since marketing began. It can be a real challenge.

The second myth represents the prevailing belief of many retail managers—advertising effectiveness equals sales results and that there is a direct relationship between advertising and sales as in Figure 1-1. Sorry, this isn't quite right either. Although advertising

Assumed relationship between advertising and sales

Figure 1-1

and sales are related, sales results alone don't nearly go far enough in helping retailers understand if their advertising is working—in fact, looking at sales alone can lead to a completely wrong conclusion!

Here's an example. You run a major (and expensive!) advertising program to promote a sales event in your store. At the end of the event, you anxiously add up the sales. By your calculation, sales volume is disappointing—you (or more importantly your manager), expected sales to be up at least 20% from the prior month, but you are up only 10%. As you get together with the rest of the managers to debrief on the event, it is agreed that the advertising did not do its job based on these results. The meeting ends with a vow by all involved to do better next time.

What retail manager hasn't been in this situation? The fact is, this is the way many retailers think about their advertising. Although this is not a totally unreasonable conclusion, it could indeed be very incorrect. Here's how. In addition to the 10% increase in sales from the prior month, what if we knew that store traffic during the promotion was actually up 30% compared to the same period last year and up 20% over the prior month. Now what would you conclude about your advertising? Obviously something didn't go quite right because the sales target was missed, but from a traffic perspective, the advertising program did draw traffic—a lot more traffic than last year or the prior month. So, as it turns out, it does appear that the advertising did its job.

"The" advertising objective

With any advertising or promotional program, first and foremost, you need to be clear about what your objective is. Stating that you want to increase sales is not especially useful. Even though the ultimate goal for most retailers is to drive sales, as mentioned, advertising alone cannot drive sales. So if advertising can't drive sales, what should the advertising objective be?

What advertising can and cannot do

In destination retail there really is only one objective you need your advertising to achieve: drive qualified prospects into your store. Period. Although this is far easier said than done, it is the one, universal advertising objective all retailers should focus on. Here's why.

Notwithstanding retailers who have Internet and telephone sales in addition to their physical "bricks and mortar" stores, the only way a sale can happen is if a prospect comes into your store. If you advertise and the number of qualified prospects that come into your store increases, then your advertising worked. If you advertise, and the number of qualified prospects coming into your store does not increase, then your advertising *may* not have worked. Wait a minute! Isn't it clear that if more prospects didn't come into my store, then my advertising DID NOT work? Not necessarily. The fact is, there are a number of factors outside of your control that can impact the traffic response of your advertising. Factors such as competitors' promotions, general business seasonality, weather conditions, changes in customer buying behavior and even broader macroeconomic factors like consumer confidence and interest rates can impact traffic. You need to analyze your traffic results in a broader context. Poor traffic results certainly suggest that your advertising program did not do its job, but you really need to think it through before you write off a campaign as ineffective.

The key is to start with the right objective—here are a few examples to consider.

Sample advertising objectives

Every retailer is different, but here are a few advertising objectives that I might want to measure against when preparing for a major advertising program:

> 1. Increase prospect traffic by 20% during the month of March compared to March last year.
>
> 2. Drive a minimum of 1,000 prospects into the showroom for Saturday's sale event.
>
> 3. Increase shopper traffic in the evening (6 PM to 9 PM daypart) by 15%.

In each example, the focus is simply to drive traffic, which is really all advertising can do. Driving traffic is the key, but of course the trick is to drive the "right" kind of traffic. Traffic for the sake of traffic isn't helpful. In fact, the "wrong" kind of traffic can actually hurt sales. For example, if you are a specialty book retailer, advertising that you'll be giving away free hot dogs to anyone who visits your store on Saturday may indeed drive traffic, but it will not likely attract qualified prospective customers. It is absolutely critical that your advertising is targeted to the right audience in message, media mix, and timing so that it will reach and resonate with real prospects.

So, advertising and sales are related, but there are a number of factors that influence the final sales result. In order to fully understand what impact their advertising is having, retailers need to measure traffic and sales conversion. Although we'll discuss sales conversion in detail in chapter 4, suffice it to say that sales conversion is essentially all those elements of retailing that help turn your prospect traffic into buyers.

As Figure 1-2 shows, there is a lot that happens between an advertising campaign and a sale. First and foremost, advertising needs to drive a traffic response. Once traffic is in the store, it needs to be converted into a sale. Sales conversion is a function of all those things that make up the shopping experience including staffing,

Actual relationship between advertising and sales

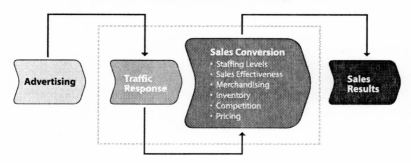

Figure 1-2

merchandising, product, pricing, *etc*. And if the retailer is effective at these, the outcome will be a sale.

Brand versus traffic response advertising

Although the ultimate goal of advertising for most retailers is to drive sales, or more accurately, to drive a positive traffic response in their store, there are other reasons for advertising beyond driving traffic. Brand advertising is usually characterized by limiting or having no specific products featured, an absence of product descriptions, and no specific "call-to-action." This type of advertising is often used when retailers want to tell the market about a community involvement initiative, perhaps announce a new staff hiring, or even communicate a new feature of their operation (*e.g.* Wonder Appliances: our salespeople are not on commission, so we serve you better). When thinking about advertising, it is useful to categorize a campaign as either a brand campaign or a traffic response campaign. Where a traffic response campaign can be measured by the prospect traffic in your store, a brand campaign cannot necessarily be measured the same way.

Brand advertising

This is advertising that communicates something about a retailer, but does not necessarily illicit a "come to my store" reaction or immediate traffic response. An example is shown in Figure 1-3. This type of advertising should not necessarily be measured by customer traffic. Though it may be that traffic increases as a result of a brand advertisement, it is not the express purpose of this type of advertising. Brand advertising is usually done to position (or re-position) a company relative to how customers perceive it or relative to other competitors. It's advertising that tries to communicate the type of retailer a company is—and who its customers are (or should be). Brand advertising is best measured by surveying customers' (or prospective customers') attitudes, opinions or perceptions before and after the brand campaign.

"Awareness" advertising

Retailers hear this frequently from their media representatives. Awareness advertising can be another way of describing brand advertising (or it's simply an over-used term for advertising that didn't drive traffic!). If you have ever bought media, you have probably heard a media representative say: "I know this advertising program will generate a significant amount of awareness for you— it's a great program and cost effective, too!"

I'm not against brand or awareness advertising—not at all. This type of advertising can be very important in predisposing prospective

Copyright © revolve furnishings

Figure 1-3

buyers to think of a particular retailer so that when they are ready to buy, they remember that retailer. However, this is still very difficult to measure. What I do question, are retailers who spend their precious advertising dollars on brand or general awareness advertising programs in the hope of driving an immediate sales response (or more accurately an immediate traffic response)—and then do it over and over and over again, even when they don't get the results they were hoping for. Retailers need to be clear about what they are trying to accomplish with their advertising. If you want to drive traffic and ultimately sales, you want to do an advertising program that will have a compelling call-to-action—something that will give prospects a really good reason to take some time out of their very busy lives to visit your store. If you're tying to create general awareness for your store or trying to create a particular image or market position for your store—great. Just don't run to the till or check the traffic count to measure the results.

Traffic response advertising

Direct marketers refer to this as "direct response," which usually

Copyright ©2004 Visions Electronics

Figure 1-4

means customers calling the advertiser by telephone or visiting their website. However, this idea is exactly the same for bricks and mortar retailers. In fact, online retailers have been measuring effectiveness based on "hits" to their website or Web traffic since the mid 90s. The physical customer traffic count in a store is the equivalent of hits to an online store. Of course, if you have an online store and telephone sales, you'll want to add this in with your store traffic counts to understand the entire traffic response (we'll cover this in *Chapter 8*).

Good traffic response advertisements usually have a clear call-to-action, telling the prospective customers exactly what you want them to do. For example, "Visit our store this weekend and save... BIG!" Good response advertisements also do a great job of creating a sense of urgency. That is, the advertisement compels the prospect to act sooner rather than later. Just like direct mail, prospects are more likely to respond to an advertisement that has a specific, and often short (*i.e.* three to ten day), time-bound deadline.

Other marketing considerations

Once you have determined what your traffic response objective is, it is absolutely critical that your advertising reach the right audience. There are many factors that will impact the effectiveness of your advertising campaign including the message, creative execution, media mix, budget and timing. If your advertising does not sufficiently reach and resonate with real prospects, you will not drive traffic. As already noted, just driving large volumes of unqualified traffic will not help, and can actually hurt, sales.

Advertising budgets

There are no hard and fast rules to setting an advertising budget. Frankly, no one is really sure how much they should spend, so don't feel too bad about being a little random on this issue. That said, determining your advertising budget isn't just picking numbers out of the air either. Here are some things you should consider.

- **Your industry**

  What you are selling will have a lot to do with how much you advertise and consequently how much you might want to spend. For example, consumer electronic retailers tend to be driven by regular and often aggressive promotions. Being in front of prospects week-in and week-out is almost a cost of doing business in this industry. This requires a very high frequency of advertising and an appropriately large budget to support it. Other industries have a very different advertising profile. For example, auto tire retailers tend to advertise at particular times of the year, such as the fall and early winter when customers are naturally thinking about buying new tires.

• Your local market

If you are a single store operator in one market, obviously you need to pay close attention to what's happening in your market. If you are a chain, you need to stay abreast of what's happening in every market in which you have a location. Every market is different. Who's advertising? How frequently? How well do they appear to be performing?

• The competition

Although most retailers generally try to keep an eye on what their competitors are doing, retailers also need to monitor what their competitors are doing from an advertising perspective. The beauty of monitoring competition this way is that all the information is readily available—just open your morning newspaper or turn on the radio. If you monitor and track what your competitors are doing in advertising, you can come up with a pretty good estimate of what they are spending. Although it's never advisable to blindly follow your competitors (what if they have it all wrong?), it is something you need to consider. In addition to understanding how much money they're spending, you'll also want to note what they are saying and how. Take particular note of the mix of products they're offering, how they are positioning themselves, and obviously their pricing. Now consider how this relates to your position and offering.

• The cost and availability of media

Every market is different from a media availability and cost perspective. How many major daily newspapers does your market have? Are there local magazines or publications?

How many radio stations? TV stations? This information is readily available—media outlets are delighted to send you their rate cards. You'll easily find all the local media listed in your local telephone directory.

- **Your financial wherewithal**

  If you open a marketing text, budgeting is often discussed in the context of concepts like "Same as last year," "All you can afford," and my favorite, "Percentage of sales." There is no magic to this—there is no formula. At the end of the day, advertising spending is a management decision. Maybe it's your decision. The financial wherewithal of your company must be considered in your decision on advertising spending. Yes, I know, you have to spend money to make money. That said, it's rarely a good idea to throw a "hail Mary pass" by spending more than you can afford in hopes of stimulating sales. You would be surprised at how far common sense can go when it comes to answering this question.

Media buying

If you have ever bought media, you know what a nerve-racking experience it can be. OK, so you have decided that you're going to try TV—after all, it's the most powerful medium on the face of the planet, right? You have reviewed your budget—you can afford it and it seems to be a sensible thing to try. Great. You call up a couple of TV stations and tell them you're interested and before you know it, you have a lineup of well-coiffed media reps at your door with slick proposals. As they start into their pitch on the exceptional targeting of their programming (which incidentally is perfect for your customer demographic—it always is), the terrific cost effectiveness on a gross rating point basis and the amazing production value that's included in your custom-designed campaign, you start to feel beads of sweat starting to form on your brow. Of course, you don't want to feel like an idiot, so you nod in tacit approval as the rep makes her closing points. You tell her you need to think about it; she tells you the program is going fast, so she'll call you tomorrow for an answer. After a day of this, you're more confused than ever, but nevertheless feel compelled to do something. If this sounds overly harsh on media reps, I don't mean it to be. Some of the best marketing people I know are media reps, and most of them are true marketing professionals with a wealth of knowledge and insight. But you need to control the process. Putting together an advertising campaign is one of the most exciting and fun things a manager gets to do. You shouldn't feel pressured or uncomfortable about doing it. After all, there's a lot at stake. Start by relaxing. Enjoy the ride! Here are a couple of tips to keep in mind when you start media buying:

- **Your objective**

  Be absolutely clear about your objective—tell your media rep what you are trying to accomplish. All together now: "MY OBJECTIVE IS TO DRIVE STORE TRAFFIC BY 25%" or whatever your traffic objective is. I guarantee you your media rep will be shocked and amazed that you have a clear objective.

- **Deals**

  Don't buy just because it's a GREAT deal or feel pressured to buy. Sometimes there are fantastic deals on media. No question. But you cannot lose sight of what your objective is. Buying media and then trying to fit an objective to it rarely ever works.

- **Relationships with media reps**

  Don't buy media because you like the rep. These sales professionals can be very compelling and very charismatic. Making a media buy because your rep gives you free tickets to a football game is not a wise strategy. No hard feelings, but it's all about you accomplishing your objectives. Media reps can be great people. In fact, over my years of buying media, I have befriended many media reps. The fact is, friend or no friend, I don't buy media on relationships and you shouldn't either. If you can get the right media buy, (*i.e.* one that you hope will help you achieve your objective), that comes first. If, at the same time, you can buy from a friend or get free tickets to a football game, that's a bonus.

- **Ask questions**

  Lots of questions. Media buying isn't a "smart contest," so ask questions. Media reps (in most cases) are very intelligent people who can teach you a lot. The only way you can learn is by asking questions. That said, media reps tend to know a lot about their particular medium, but may not know much about other media, or for obvious reasons don't want to talk a lot about other media. I think it's always a good idea to meet with media reps from several different media in your market. For example, even if you don't intend to use outdoor advertising, it might be worth your time to hear what the outdoor media rep has to say. Frankly, media reps will be quite happy to explain things to you.

Working with ad agencies

Some people have had excellent experiences working with ad agencies and some have had very bad experiences. I have experienced both. All things considered, I think it's a good idea to work with an agency. That said, I don't recommend you disengage from the process and let the agency call the shots. Agencies often have a whole host of experts—from media buying, campaign strategy development and especially creative services—but like hiring any professional service, you need to be an informed buyer and a "good" client. Agencies love good clients. What's a good client, you ask? A good client is a client who is clear about what they are trying to do (*i.e.* have a clearly defined objective—note the reoccurring theme here). Besides having a clearly stated objective, a good client is also someone who has an open mind, is engaged and thoughtful, asks questions and challenges the agency. Good clients want great value, but are willing to pay for great work. If you're really watching your budget (and who isn't?), ask your agency what you can do yourself internally—just like those TV shows on home renovating where homeowners are looking to save some expense by removing their old porch themselves. You can do the same with an advertising agency. And lastly, don't be afraid to ask how much it will all cost—agencies are happy to give you the gory details.

Campaign timing

Every business has seasonality—yours does too. Most retailers understand this intuitively. Campaign timing is simply the process of determining when you will launch a campaign or allocate your advertising throughout the year. Traffic volume and patterns can tell you a lot about when prospects are predisposed to shop in your store. It's also a good idea to look at annual sales by week and month—when are customers coming into your store and when are they buying. Again this is not rocket science—start by plotting these things on a calendar and you'll be well on your way.

Targeting and segmentation

Getting more prospects into your store is the objective, but you need the right prospects. Driving traffic levels up significantly can actually HURT sales as tire kickers and other "traffic noise" plug your aisles or squander your sales staff's precious time. Targeting and segmentation are nothing more than identifying who your likely customers are. Start by looking at who has already purchased—age, gender, where they live, what they bought, and so forth. Also, if you sell goods produced by manufacturers, ask them for information on the demographics of who their products are targeted at—in most cases all this work as already been done by the manufacturers and usually they are quite willing to share this information with their retail partners.

Creative execution

Open your morning newspaper and have a look at the ads. See the ones that are cluttered, confusing, poorly laid out and by and large unpleasing to the eye? You've probably just found a "do-it-yourself" advertiser. Everyone believes they have good sensibilities about what an advertisement (print, broadcast, outdoor, *etc.*) should look or sound like. And why shouldn't we all? On a daily basis every one of us consumes vast quantities of advertising and as a result we all have opinions on what we like and don't like. Unfortunately, creating an ad you like and creating an effective ad are not always the same thing. In truth, there are established principals for developing good creative and most people don't know them. The problem is that advertising is utterly subjective. Everyone has an opinion of what good and bad advertising is. If there is one area that I recommend retailers get professional help with, it's on creative. Why bother spending money on advertising when your ads don't get read or heard? I would trade a larger media buy and weak creative for strong creative and a smaller media buy in a heart beat. You should too. Does this mean you need to hire an ad agency? Not necessarily. If you do a lot of print advertising, hiring a graphic designer on a contract basis or as a regular employee will be one of the best investments you could make. You can hire an excellent graphic designer on a project basis or as a permanent fixture for a lot less than you might think. For broadcast media (TV and radio), you really need to work with the pros—either the media's own creative people or through an agency.

Advertising and traffic patterns

If your advertising is working, you should expect to see some impact on store traffic. When you monitor traffic in your store consistently, you will be able to see clearly the results of your advertising.

Starting at a very basic level, if we compare two promotions, we can see the impact on traffic of each promotion. In promotion A shown in Figure 1-5 traffic levels have increased compared to the traffic levels prior to and after the promotional period.

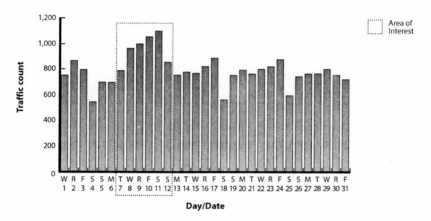

Figure 1-5

In promotion B shown in Figure 1-6, traffic levels have not increased during the promotion, compared to the traffic levels prior to and following the promotional period. In this case, it appears as though promotion B had little or no impact on traffic.

Looking at traffic patterns like this, compared to your advertising and promotional efforts, can very quickly tell you how effective

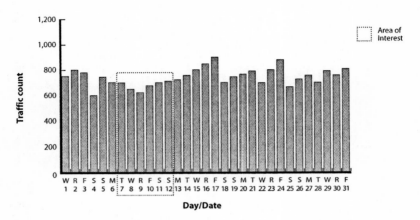

Traffic response to Promotion B

Figure 1-6

your advertising was at accomplishing its objective. Now of course, there could be many other factors that influence traffic levels, but advertising is a good place to start.

Successful campaigns—seeing results

Here is an example of a campaign that was effective in driving customer traffic. As the chart in Figure 1-7 shows, traffic ramped up at the beginning of the campaign and peaked on the Saturday of the event.

The average daily traffic was up 45% from the prior week, and the Saturday of the promotion was up 85% compared to the prior five Saturdays as seen in the chart in Figure 1-8. Following the promotion, traffic levels subsided to normal, average levels similar to those prior to the promotion. As a retail marketing manager, this is precisely the kind of traffic response I would want to see during a major advertising campaign or promotion. Based on this traffic data, I would declare this campaign to be successful (of course I would need to compare this to year-over-year results to be sure this isn't just normal seasonality).

In this next example, again traffic was up significantly during the

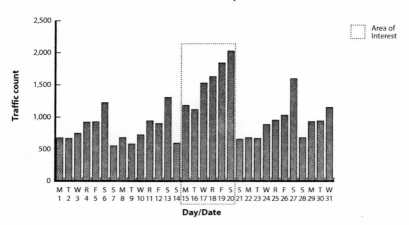

Figure 1-7

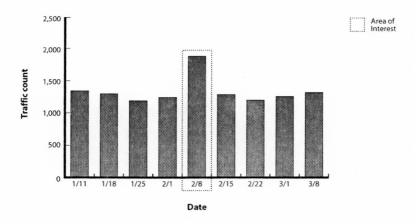

Figure 1-8

promotional period as shown in Figure 1-9. Specifically, traffic was up 43% over the average day prior to the promotion, and up

40% compared to the average traffic post promotion. Clearly this promotion drove traffic during the promotional period, but to truly understand the results, retailers need to also consider business seasonality—in other words, what was traffic for this same period last year?

Even though traffic appears to be favorably up, when compared to the prior year, we may learn that traffic is only up marginally, or not

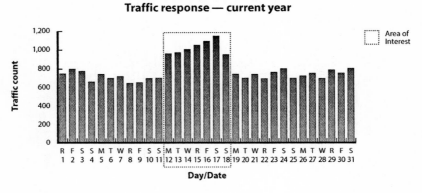

Figure 1-9

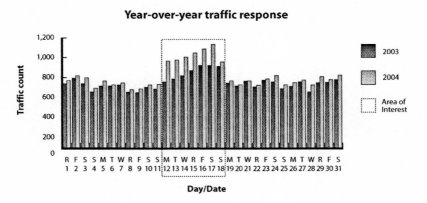

Figure 1-10

up at all! As the year-over-year traffic chart in Figure 1-10 reveals, traffic is indeed up year-over-year and we can confidently conclude that our advertising program had a positive impact.

It is critically important to compare apples-to-apples as much as possible. Traffic variations month-to-month could simply represent changes in business seasonality—that is, it may not be at all unusual for April traffic to be lower than March, but if April this year had lower traffic than April last year, that may be an issue.

Here's another example, this time illustrating the impact of a one-day event. As Figure 1-11 clearly shows, traffic was up dramatically. Again, from an advertising perspective, it is not hard to conclude that this advertising did its job. Call your media rep up and tell them that you're delighted with the results—they'll be shocked (and relieved).

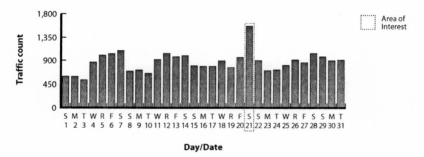

Figure 1-11

When campaigns don't work—seeing the lack of results

Taking the other extreme, here is a series of campaigns a retailer undertook that didn't have the same kind of traffic response. As you can see in Figure 1-12, there is no apparent change in traffic response as a result of this advertising. In fact, traffic actually went down some weeks when the campaign was running!

As we follow another campaign in Figure 1-13, the results don't seem to change. The traffic response is modest or non-existent.

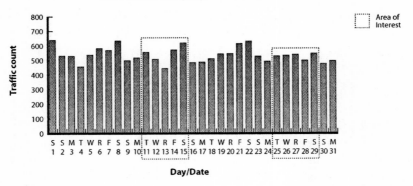

Figure 1-12

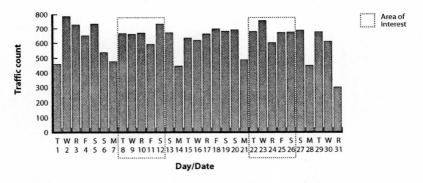

Figure 1-13

By looking at these traffic patterns, it's impossible to conclude anything other than these campaigns were not working. When we discussed the apparently poor traffic performance, it was even more incredible that the retail manager, who was responsible for these campaigns, was concerned about making any changes. Surprisingly, he was still nervous about altering the campaign—"These results are disappointing, but how much worse would they be if I changed my advertising?" I told this manager that I wouldn't be concerned about changing the campaign—but I would be terrified of continuing it! Clearly this was not working. Even taking the advertising funds and putting them on the bottom line would likely have been a better business decision. I just don't buy the excuse that things could always be worse. The fact is, merely speculating about outcomes without any data is extremely reckless.

I know, I know—most of you reading this are thinking that this manager is just not very competent. However, before you pass judgment, you would be surprised at how many very smart retailers spend money on advertising and don't have the faintest clue about what's working or not. I'd say it's the majority.

The fact is, every retailer has had ad campaigns that bombed—and don't worry, you will have more in the future—I guarantee it. It's not a crime to run a campaign that in the end doesn't work. However, it should be a crime to run ineffective campaign after campaign after campaign, squandering precious resources. If something doesn't seem to work, experiment. Experimenting is a great way to understand what works best—how else are you going to figure it out? That said, experimentation without measurement is just foolish. Without a measure, you're flying blind. You simply cannot say what's working and what's not. Traffic patterns can provide you with tremendous insight about what works and what doesn't—it's really not that hard.

So back to the poor retailer who didn't want to change his ineffective advertising. The good news is that he's now looking at traffic data and is not afraid to try things that have a demonstrable impact on his traffic. It's a happy ending.

Traffic is up—or is it? Drilling down on traffic patterns to get the true insights

Just looking at general traffic patterns like the previous examples can, indeed, tell you a lot about how your advertising is performing. However, sometimes things aren't always what they appear to be. The traffic chart in Figure 1-14 shows traffic levels on the days this retailer dropped flyers. As you can see, every Wednesday that they dropped a flyer, traffic "spiked"—38% versus the average prior

Wednesday on flyer #1 and 47% versus the average Wednesday on flyer # 2—Wow! What terrific results!

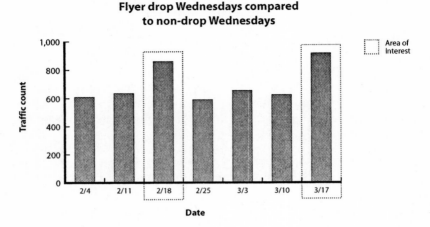

Flyer drop Wednesdays compared to non-drop Wednesdays

Figure 1-14

We were pretty excited about the results—everyone likes to see a success story. But before we popped the champagne, we thought we had better take a closer look at the traffic data. The flyers were dropped on Wednesdays, so naturally we wanted to understand what was happening to traffic on Thursday, Friday, Saturday and Sunday (these flyer events always lasted from Wednesday to Sunday).

The traffic chart below shows what the traffic levels were during the promotion days (*i.e.* Wednesday through Sunday) versus the average traffic for a Wednesday through Sunday during non-promotional weeks. As the chart in Figure 1-15 shows, clearly traffic was up during every day during the promotion compared to the non-promotion weeks. So far so good. Start chilling the champagne!

Just to be on the safe side, we thought we had better run the same analysis on the second campaign. What do you know—the same pattern. As the chart in Figure 1-16 below shows, like the first campaign, traffic is up across all days during the second promotion. This is really starting to look good.

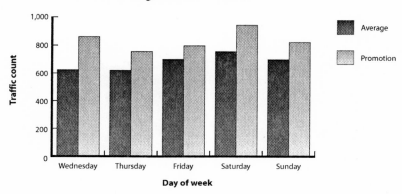

Comparison of promotion traffic to average traffic— Promotion 1

Figure 1-15

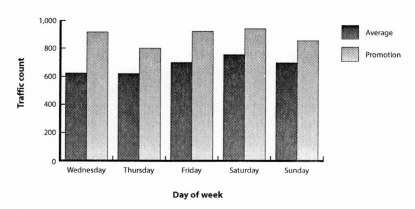

Comparison of promotion traffic to average traffic—Promotion 2

Figure 1-16

There was only one more thing to look at—traffic patterns AFTER the campaign. Although we would expect traffic to fall back to average levels after the campaign, it is possible that the traffic levels might have stayed slightly higher, suggesting that there may be a "sustaining" affect. What we discovered is shown in Figure 1-17—traffic levels following the campaigns dropped significantly. In fact, traffic dropped so much that the huge traffic gains realized during the promotional weeks were dramatically reduced when the weeks following the promotions were considered.

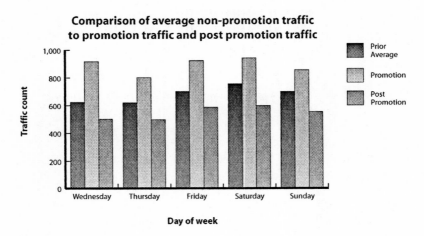

Comparison of average non-promotion traffic to promotion traffic and post promotion traffic

Figure 1-17

Unfortunately, there'll be no champagne corks popping for this promotion! But what we did learn is that you need to take a longer view of advertising effectiveness as it relates to traffic in order to understand if you're generating incremental traffic or simply shifting existing traffic. Fundamentally, retailers generally believe that when they run a promotion that they will attract incremental or additional prospects into their stores. However, as this previous example shows, sometimes advertising may simply shift prospect traffic. If the net effect of your advertising is to shift customers to come in sooner than they might have otherwise done, then you might not be getting the results you had hoped—even if it appears as though your advertising is effectively driving traffic.

On the other hand, shifting customer traffic forward may indeed be a good strategic decision. For example, if you knew that a competitor was about to hold a major sales event or planning a grand opening, it may make perfect sense to use advertising to drive customers into your store sooner (*i.e.* before your competitor launches their campaign), even if the net amount of incremental traffic is modest.

What media best drives traffic?

If your advertising is working, you should expect to see some impact on store traffic. When you monitor traffic in your store consistently, you will be able to see the results of your advertising quite clearly.

Although some media tend to be better at, or used more often for, traffic response advertising than others, before I start receiving nasty letters from media reps, it is important to note that virtually any medium could be used to drive a retail traffic response. However, based on our experience in monitoring retail campaigns and traffic, we have concluded that certain media are more effective at driving traffic than others. As previously mentioned, in addition to media mix, other campaign components such as creative execution and media weight (*i.e.* the size of your media buy) will influence the traffic response as well.

Table 1-1 provides a quick comparative overview of various media's ability to stimulate a traffic response, and the following section will provide a more detailed review of media characteristics.

- **Daily Newspaper**

    Newspaper is the undisputed champ of retail advertising. Newspapers have several great advantages as a traffic response medium. First, by its very nature (*i.e.* daily) it has a sense of urgency and implicitly suggests "Come in today." Furthermore, newspaper enables advertisers to communicate detailed information without compromising the power of the ad—important pieces of information like stores hours, price points and even detailed product descriptions can be included. Newspapers also have relatively short lead times (usually several days or a week prior to publication), modest production requirements and relatively low cost. The samples in Figure 1-18 are good examples of typical newspaper ads.

- **Magazines**

    Magazines tend to have long "shelf lives" and cover larger geographic areas—provincial, state or national. Magazines

Table 1-1

Media comparison by cost & ability to drive traffic response

Medium	Cost	Ability to drive traffic	Comments
Newspapers	Low to medium	**Very Good**	The undisputed leader in retailing, the majority of retail ad budgets are spent on newspapers.
Flyers/ Circulars	Medium	**Very Good**	A favorite of retail, flyers and circulars offer flexibility and impact all with the immediacy and distribution of a daily newspaper.
Direct Mail	Low	**Very Good**	Direct mail can be very effective for driving a traffic response. Effectiveness usually depends on the quality of the mailing list.
Radio	Low to medium	**Good**	Radio is a terrific "take action" medium and is used extensively as a support medium.
Television	High in absolute terms, but low on a cost-per-prospect reached basis, especially when used nationally	**Good**	Very powerful medium but long lead times, production costs, and high frequency may make it prohibitive for smaller retailers.
Magazines	Medium to high	**Poor**	Long lead times and relatively modest circulation make magazines a less popular choice with retailers for traffic response campaigns.
Outdoor	Medium	**Poor**	Although outdoor is great for general awareness and brand building, it is used less for immediate traffic response campaigns in part due to the extended exposure—outdoor space is often sold in 4 week blocks.

Copyright © Freedom Ford Sales and Copyright ©2003-2004 Mobler Furniture

Figure 1-18

usually have long lead times (*i.e.* you need to get them your artwork well before the publication date). This is not typically the kind of medium you would use to create urgency and consequently tends not to be a good choice for immediate traffic response. That said, it may make a lot of sense as part of a broader national campaign to support traffic response activities.

• Television

Television can be a very powerful traffic response medium. Although fleeting, TV messages with the use of sound and image can be every compelling. However, TV ad frequency usually needs to be very high in order to deliver the message to the intended audience, and consequently, cost can be a factor. Also, production can be costly and the lead times are usually quite long (weeks or even months). Although the cost is comparatively high relative to other media, it can be extremely cost effective nationally because of its broad reach.

• Radio

Following close to newspaper advertising, radio is the retailers' second choice. Radio can deliver immediacy to a campaign and the relatively short production and scheduling lead times give retailers plenty of flexibility. The only downside is that radio has content limitations. You can only effectively communicate a small amount of information in a thirty second message, and because the message is fleeting you need to keep it very simple and say it often. Radio can be a terrific support medium or it can work on its own.

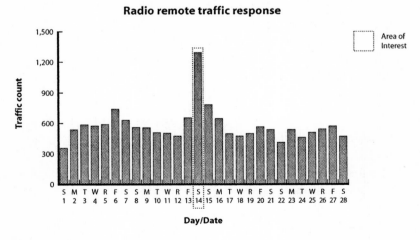

Radio remote traffic response

Figure 1-19

Radio remotes can also be very effective when used sparingly. A radio remote is where the radio station broadcasts "live" from your store location. This creates a sense of "event" and can be very effective in attracting prospects to your location. The chart in Figure 1-19 is an example of what impact a radio remote can have on traffic.

- **Outdoor**

Also referred to as billboards, outdoor advertising is a category of media that includes all shapes and varieties of outdoor signs, posters, murals, even the sides of buses! Although this is not a first choice, it can work as a support medium for a traffic response advertising campaign. Because outdoor advertising is usually sold in minimum four-week periods, your campaign needs to last that long. This detracts

Copyright ©2004 Hartco Corporation

Figure 1-20

---

from the immediacy—why hurry in, if I have a month to get there?

• **Flyers/Circulars**

Flyers are a major part of the retail advertising landscape. Flyers can be delivered either on their own or inserted into a daily newspaper. For the most part, flyers can be very effective at driving a traffic response. When inserted into major daily newspapers, flyers get the benefit and targeted distribution of the newspaper, but allow the retailers to really standout with the flyer size, layout and color of their choice. Also, flyers are generally associated with sales events, so the consumer response to this medium is usually immediate—whether there's a sales event or not.

• **Direct Mail**

Though used more sparingly by retailers, a direct mail campaign can be very effective in driving a traffic response. The key, as with all direct mail, is the list. Sending mail to an existing base of customers can work very well; however, sending out "acquisition" mail or letters to "cold" prospects either as addressed or unaddressed mail is usually significantly less effective.

Advertising in multiple markets

If you have stores in multiple markets or even multiple stores in the same market, keep reading. The fact is, a successful advertising program in one market doesn't necessarily guarantee success in another, or even among stores in the same market. It's not really that hard to understand why. Every market has different characteristics: population demographics, competitive environment, media availability, and potentially different store characteristics. All these factors can influence the traffic response to an advertising campaign.

As the charts in Figures 1-21 and 1-22 show, the campaign in market A had a material impact on traffic levels in this store. However, the same campaign in market B at exactly the same time had a very different outcome.

A campaign may be deemed successful even if traffic doesn't go up in every location; however, the net aggregate traffic response should

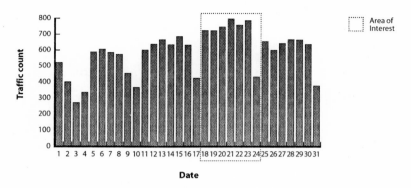

Figure 1-21

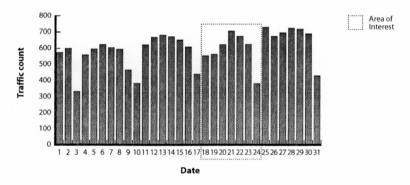

Figure 1-22

be positive. If an advertising campaign doesn't have a similarly positive impact in different markets (or locations), the key is to figure out what will drive traffic in the under-responding market or store. Although more complicated from a marketing management standpoint, it may be far more effective from a traffic response perspective to run a different media mix, message or weight in one market than in others. For example, a chain might run newspaper ads in one market, a flyer in a second market and radio in a third. This may seem extreme and possibly costly in terms of economies of scale, but there really is no point in spending money on advertising if it doesn't result in a material traffic response. Clearly the cost/benefit of this type of approach would need to be evaluated.

Too much of a good thing: Can you advertise too much?

Some retailers follow a very regular advertising pattern. For example, they will drop sales flyers every Friday of every week in the year. As the traffic chart in Figure 1-23 shows, it is very difficult to determine precisely what impact this intensive (and costly) advertising activity is having on traffic. Are the flyers driving a positive traffic

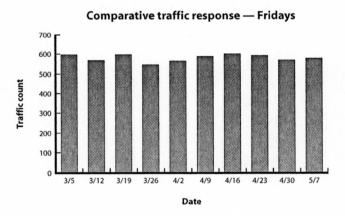

Figure 1-23

response? Is it overkill? Would eliminating one or a few of the flyers have any effect on the traffic response profile at all?

In this situation, the only way to know for sure is to change the schedule and see what happens. To this I often get a "If it ain't broke don't fix it" reaction. Or "we tried that once and sales went down." Unless you do this and carefully analyze the results, you will never know for certain. Just like the advertiser who continued to run ineffective campaign after ineffective campaign, this is really no different. I suspect that retailers who run these non-stop campaigns may be able to save money if they cut back on some of those flyers. If they did eliminate some of these flyers, they would have a budget surplus that could be reallocated to experimental advertising to see if something else might drive more traffic. Or it could be used to fund merchandising programs, staff training, or even something really crazy like improving profitability! But they won't know if they don't try. Could retailers who continuously advertise save money and not materially impact traffic and sales? Probably, yes. Unfortunately, this isn't a situation in which most retailers find themselves, but it can happen.

Although there is a risk to experimenting (*i.e.* not running ads to see what happens), I would suggest that the value of knowing what happens would probably outweigh the potential risk of a short-term experiment. It could very well make sense to advertise every week, but I'm skeptical. And given the high cost of advertising, I'm just not convinced that blindly dropping flyers or running newspaper ads week-after-week is the answer.

Chapter Summary

- Advertising is the primary mechanism retailers use to drive traffic into their stores—especially the new prospects who are critically important to any retailer who wants to grow their business. Not only is advertising critically important to driving the business, it's also very expensive, which means your advertising decisions also greatly impact the bottom line as well as the top line.

- Although many retailers don't think you can practically measure advertising or that sales is the only measure, the fact is you can, and the best measure is traffic, not sales.

- The key to understanding advertising effectiveness is in having a clear objective—specifically, retailers need a traffic response objective. Once you're clear about that, the whole issue of measuring advertising effectiveness becomes a much less abstract concept. That said, there still is a lot of trial and error and subjectivity about all the decisions that go into an ad campaign—creative execution, media mix, budget, timing, etc. As long as you measure against your traffic objective, you may go wrong, but you won't go too far wrong—at least not for long. If traffic isn't going up, there's a good chance your advertising isn't working. Don't be afraid to try something else.

- Everyone believes they have good marketing sensibilities. Know your limitations. Get help when you need it—especially from a creative execution perspective. Don't hesitate to work with ad agencies, but don't be afraid to find out what it costs before you begin and stay engaged—it's your business! In other words, be a good client.

- The traffic response to advertising and promotions can be very apparent in the number and timing of prospects in your store. If a campaign is very successful, you should see a measurable traffic response—relative to both current traffic trends and year-over-year. When advertising doesn't work, you can see that too.

- Before you discard a particular campaign based on traffic results, make sure you have thought through all the factors that might have impacted traffic. For example, if you ran a campaign during a major snowstorm, the campaign itself might have been just fine and it was this extenuating circumstance that suppressed the traffic response.

- All media can drive traffic to an extent. However, some media tend to be better suited to traffic stimulation that others.

- For retailers with stores in multiple markets, careful attention needs to be paid to the traffic responses across the chain. A campaign in one market may not have the same impact as in another market.

- Lastly, for retailers who continuously advertise (*e.g.* dropping flyers every week), there may be cost savings by selectively cutting back on advertising. By doing this carefully, retailers might find they spend less without negatively impacting traffic or sales.

CHAPTER

Setting and Refining Store Hours

Do prospects and customers visit your store because of your store hours or despite them?

Setting and Refining Store Hours

UNFORTUNATELY, THERE ARE no hard and fast rules for setting store operation hours—too bad. It's too bad because it's an area that vexes retailers of all sizes in virtually every category. The whole idea of setting store hours seems to fall into the category of common sense—set store hours that are convenient for customers. It's just that simple, isn't it? Mostly the answer is yes, but there are nuances about setting and refining store hours that should be considered.

There is no question that store hours have been getting longer and longer as retailers try to find any edge over the competition. Meanwhile, customers are expecting retailers to be open at times that are convenient for their lifestyles.

STORE HOURS

- Setting store hours
- Using traffic data in store hour decisions
- Consequences of changing store hours
- Multi-locations

Extended hours, Sundays and holidays—customers expect more and retailers are giving more. Understanding prospect traffic volume and timing in your store can provide important clues about what your store hours should be. In this chapter we will explore exactly how you can use traffic data to determine store hours. First, we'll briefly review the different ways retailers set store hours and the different circumstances that lead retailers to change or modify store hours. Although you would think this would be one of the more static variables in retailing (and it is), store hours do and probably should change periodically.

Next, we will look specifically at how traffic analysis can help management set and refine store hours. Along the way, we'll look at the case of a retailer extending store hours, and we'll touch on the idea of store hour experimentation and how traffic data can be used to help understand results.

Lastly, we'll address the consequences of changing store hours and identify some of the unique challenges that multi-location retailers face in this regard.

Setting store hours

Setting store hours is one of the most fundamental decisions retailers make, but it's a more complex decision than many might expect. Virtually all retailers are open Monday through Friday from 10 AM to 5 PM—so far, so good. Invariably decisions about store hours come down to those one or two hours prior to 10 AM and those two or three hours after 5 PM. Of course, setting hours for weekends, holidays and special events is a separate issue. In all cases, however, there are a number of factors retailers should consider when setting or refining store hours.

Customer feedback

Always a good place to start, polling customers to get a sense of what they find convenient is advisable. Of course, be careful not to over-react to this input. It may be convenient to be open from 7 AM until 11 PM every night based on when customers *say* they would like to shop, but clearly this would not be practical, and frankly, not likely when these customers would actually shop. Instead of asking customers literally what they would like your store hours to be, try to get them to describe their behaviors relative to shopping visits in your store.

Competitive pressure

The starting point is to list your key competitors and then document what the store hours are for each of them. If you're really keen, you might even visit your key competitors' stores to get a sense of their traffic volume, especially during the early hours and near closing hours—that is, during the hours you may not be open but may be considering. For example, if you surveyed your top three competitors and determined that they were opened for 6, 8 and 14 hours more per week respectively than your store, you might want to consider extending your store hours. Think of it this way: if a competitor has 6 more selling hours in a week than you do, over the course of a year that adds up to 312 more selling hours! If during some of these 312 hours some of your very loyal customers visit your competitor simply because your store isn't open, you might want to think about extending your hours.

Property covenants

Most shopping malls and some retail centers have, as part of the lease, an agreement that all retailers be open for specific hours. Even though there may be some flexibility, generally, retailers will need to conform to the store hour covenants imposed by the property manager.

Seasonality

Although standard store hours may not vary much, every business is subject to some kind of business seasonality. Seasonality is just another way to characterize the peaks and valleys of the business cycle to which all retailers are subject. For example, back-to-school represents an important season for many kinds of retailers; for other retailers, Mother's Day is one of the busiest times. I think you get the idea. The point is retailers often do change (usually extending) store hours to take advantage of seasonal busy times.

Holidays and special events

Retail shoppers have come to expect a change in store hours during holidays. Whether these are extended hours or reduced hours, retail shoppers understand that holidays will often mean a change in store hours. Of course, special events which are driven by the retailer themselves represent another circumstance where retailers may modify store hours. For example, a retailer might hold a "Midnight Madness" event and literally keep the store open until this traditionally unusual retail hour.

Now that we have reviewed some of the more common factors that influence store hours, we'll turn our attention to how you can apply traffic analysis to setting and refining those hours.

Using traffic analysis to refine store hours

Instead of relying upon intuition or just plain old history to set operating hours (*i.e.* this is the way we've always been and we don't see any need to change it), retailers need a more reliable method. They need a system that is reliable, consistent and accurate enough to identify changes, sometimes subtle changes, in their business. The assumptions and reasons store hours might have been set initially (maybe even many years earlier) may not apply today. The market is changing; customers and competitors are changing. You have been changing as well.

In this section we will explore what traffic data can tell you about store hours. Are you closing too soon? Are you opening too late? Too early? Was it worth extending store hours for the big sale?

General traffic patterns

The first step in the process is to simply understand what your

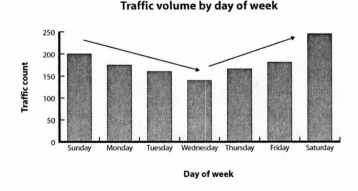

Figure 2-1

traffic patterns are. Naturally, you will need to understand traffic volume by hour and as well as by the day of the week. Traffic patterns may be very consistent or they can vary dramatically. As the chart in Figure 2-1 demonstrates, traffic volumes and patterns can and do vary by day.

By analyzing traffic volumes by day of week, we get a sense of when the busiest days are. The next step is to drill down to the hourly traffic level. Generally, hourly traffic patterns fall into one of three categories: front-end loaded, normally distributed or back-end loaded.

Front-end loaded

As shown in Figure 2-2, a front-end loaded traffic pattern is one in which traffic volumes are highest at the early part of the day and then decrease as the day progresses. In this example, traffic peaks between 9 AM and 11 AM and is essentially flat from 1 PM until closing. Not only does this pattern have obvious staffing implications, it also begs for an answer to what traffic might be from 8 AM to 9 AM (*i.e.* an hour earlier than the store currently opens).

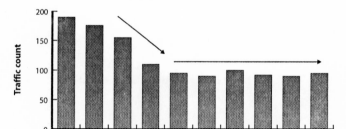

Front-end loaded traffic distribution

Figure 2-2

Normal distribution

A traffic pattern that follows a normal distribution has traffic start low at opening, ramp up through the day and then decrease until close.

Peak traffic volume usually occurs between 11 AM and 2 PM. The chart in Figure 2-3 shows a typical normally distributed traffic pattern.

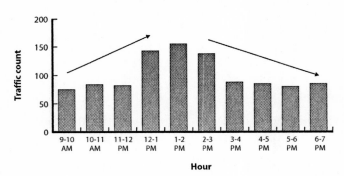

Normally distributed traffic pattern

Figure 2-3

Back-end loaded

As the name suggests, a back-end loaded traffic pattern is one in which traffic is lowest at opening and then ramps up throughout the day. The traffic peak tends to be at, or very near, the end of the day as shown in Figure 2-4.

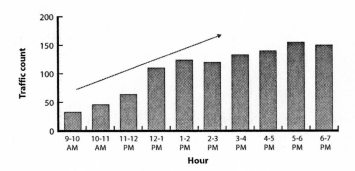

Back-end loaded traffic distribution

Figure 2-4

Hourly traffic patterns and store hours

As these general hourly traffic distribution charts show, traffic volumes, especially at the beginning and end of the day, can provide invaluable insight about store hours. For example, in the front-end loaded distribution, it might make sense to open the store earlier. Conversely, in the back-end loaded distribution, it might make sense to extend hours beyond the current closing hour. Let's look at a specific example to illustrate the point.

London Antiques: A case study in maximizing the traffic opportunity by revising store hours

London Antiques is a single location antique retailer. After analyzing traffic data for the past several months, management identified the typical weekday and hourly traffic distribution. As the chart in Figure 2-5 shows, London Antiques has a back-end loaded hourly traffic distribution.

Based on the hourly traffic distribution, management wondered whether the store hours were optimal. Although store hours of 9 AM to 6 PM seemed to make sense over the years, perhaps it was time for a change? Based on the traffic patterns, management hypothesized that extending store hours by two additional hours could make sense given that the last hour of the day had such strong traffic.

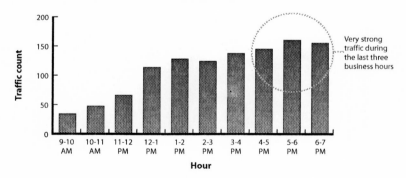

Figure 2-5

There was one small problem with the idea—staff expense. Experimenting with extending store hours seemed like the right thing to do, but what about the extra two hours of staff expense? Although management was interested in the outcome of a test, there was no appetite (or budget) for additional staff. After further consideration, management decided to conduct the test in such a way that staff expenses would not be affected. Given that the early hours had comparatively low traffic counts compared to the ending hours, management decided to open the store two hours later and close two hours later. By shifting the operating hours, the total staff expense would remain unchanged, but, if management was right, the store would actually receive more prospect traffic.

After about a month, a new hourly traffic distribution emerged. As seen in the chart in Figure 2-6, the new, extended store hours appear to be a win. Prior to the store hour change, average traffic counts from 9 AM to 10 AM and 10 AM to 11 AM were 33 and 46 counts respectively. During the extended store hours, traffic counts were 140 between 6 PM and 7 PM and 92 between 7 PM and 8 PM. By modifying the store hours, London Antiques traded 79 prospect counts at the beginning of the day for 154 prospect counts at the end of the day. The net effect of making this change in store hours was an increase in total traffic of 95% for the 2 hours. And what's

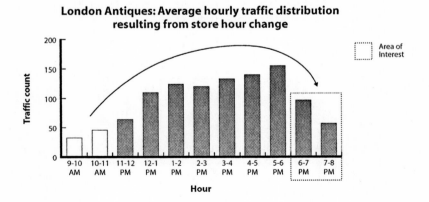

Figure 2-6

really magical is that it was achieved without incurring additional staff expense because total operating hours did not increase.

Extending store hours means more business, right?

One common assumption about extending store hours is that it will lead to incremental traffic and consequently incremental sales. It makes sense, doesn't it? If your store is currently open for 8 hours and you decide to stay open one additional hour, you should get all the traffic you normally would have during the 8 hours plus extra traffic from the new, extra hour. Unfortunately, this isn't always what happens. Here's a case to illustrate the point.

Growing the store hours: A case study in extending store hours

In an effort to take advantage of the active spring planting season, Gail Greenwood, owner of Greenwood's Greenhouse and Garden Center, decided to extend store hours by one additional hour. Store hours were already long at this time of the year—8 AM to 9 PM, but the way Gail figured it, as long as customers wanted to buy, the store should be open. As a seasonal business, you have to make the sales when you can. Gail was convinced that remaining open for an additional hour would more than cover the incremental expense of

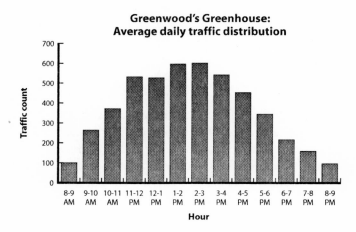

Figure 2-7

paying staff to work the extra hour. Moreover, staying open would provide more convenience to customers. In Gail's mind it was virtually a no-brainer.

Prior to extending store hours, the average traffic distribution by hour was as illustrated in the chart in Figure 2-7. Although traffic did ramp down through the evening hours, there still were 96 prospect counts from 8 PM to the 9 PM closing.

Gail extended the store hours by one extra hour to 10 PM and promoted this to customers through large signs at the entrance and exit of store. The chart in Figure 2-8 shows the average traffic by hour after several weeks with extended hours.

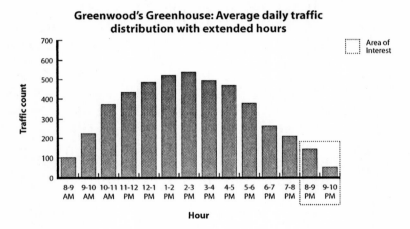

Figure 2-8

Interestingly, evening traffic did actually increase with the extended hours. The new extended hour was receiving some 52 prospects. Gail thought this was a pretty good result. Given Gail's relatively high average sale value and conversion rate, these extra 52 prospects more than paid for the additional staff expense of keeping the store open for an additional hour.

Before Gail cracks open a bottle of champagne to celebrate the successful business decision however, she should look at the data a little more closely. It is true that evening traffic has increased, and that the new 9 PM to 10 PM hour is generating 52 prospect counts on average.

So far so good. But if we look at the total traffic for the day, we realize it hasn't increased—in fact, it decreased. Prior to the extended store hours, the average daily traffic was 4,806 counts; after extending store hours the average daily traffic was 4,757 counts—that's 49 fewer counts than before! How could this be possible?

Here's how. The fundamental assumption that Gail and many other retailers make is that extending store hours will lead to incremental traffic—period. It does not seem probable to retailers that by extending store hours, the result would simply be a shift in traffic timing and that the overall volume would not materially increase. But that is exactly what happened at Greenwood's Greenhouse and Garden Center and it's what happens to many retailers. Total traffic did not increase (actually it decreased slightly), but traffic timing did shift to the evening hours. In this situation, Gail actually increased her staff expense by 1 hour, but didn't generate any incremental traffic. Assuming that sales conversion rates and average sale values remained constant, this was not a good decision. The chart in Figure 2-9 and Table 2-1 below provide a comparative view of traffic by hour before and after the change in store hours. With traffic data, this type of analysis is a straightforward exercise, and the true impact of a change in store hours becomes clear.

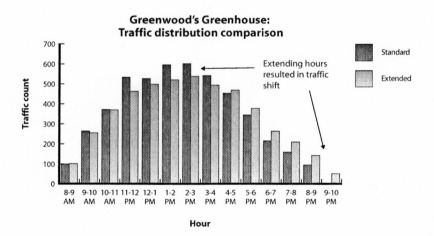

Figure 2-9

Table 2-1

Greenwood's Greenhouse: Hourly traffic count comparison

Hour	Original Hours	Extended Hours	Traffic Change
8 to 9 AM	100	101	1
9 to 10 AM	264	255	-9
10 to 11 AM	372	370	-2
11 to 12 PM	533	463	-70
12 to 1 PM	527	499	-28
1 to 2 PM	597	521	-76
2 to 3 PM	602	538	-64
3 to 4 PM	542	494	-48
4 to 5 PM	453	469	16
5 to 6 PM	345	378	33
6 to 7 PM	216	264	48
7 to 8 PM	159	210	51
8 to 9 PM	96	143	47
9 to 10 PM	n/a	52	52
Total	**4,806**	**4,757**	**-49**

Consequences of changing store hours

Changing store hours is a big decision and it shouldn't be taken lightly. As the prior example showed, changing store hours can have a direct impact on operating expenses. As part of the decision to change store hours, there are a number of considerations retailers should keep in mind.

Advertising and communications

Choosing to change your store hours is not as easy as updating the store hour sign on your front door (or wherever you display store hours). It takes some time for customers and prospects to realize that your hours have changed. To an extent, you need to "shout" the store hour change. Large, bold signage at the front of the door is an obvious and effective first step. In order to improve your chances of attracting incremental traffic versus shifting existing traffic, including a strong message in all advertising and communications is advised.

Staff expenses

As the Greenwood's Greenhouse case study showed, there is a financial consequence of extending (or reducing) store hours. Retailers need to understand what the staffing (or more specifically, the staff expense) consequences are of changing store hours. In addition to the financial consequences, there are other issues to keep in mind. For example, if you extend hours significantly and do not increase your total staff numbers (*i.e.* get existing staff to work longer), you run the risk of burning out your staff, which could lead to turnover. On the other hand, if you reduce hours, you might find that staff aren't getting enough hours and consequently leave to earn more elsewhere.

Customer confusion

Shoppers like familiarity. Constant tinkering with store hours is not advisable, as you run the risk of confusing prospects and customers. "Why is the store closed? I was here last month and they were open at 9 AM, now they're not. What's up with these guys?"

Competitive response

A good reason to extend store hours may be to create a competitive advantage. For example, if yours is the only golf equipment store open 7 days a week from 9 AM to 9 PM, you might find that you have a slight advantage over your competitors who are open only 6 days a week from 9 AM to 6 PM. In this case, the extended hours may make a lot of sense (again assuming you're not just shifting existing traffic). The only issue you need to keep in mind is that this competitive advantage is not sustainable. That is, any one of your competitors can easily extend their store hours to match yours. And if by doing so, the impact on your business decreases your total traffic, you end up with higher staff expenses supporting fewer prospects—not a good trade.

Refining store hours for multiple locations

As this chapter has shown so far, setting and refining store hours can be tricky—there are a number of factors to consider and sometimes what you expect will happen doesn't. Everything that we just covered about store hour changes naturally applies to multi-location chains with the addition of a couple of nuances. This next section will discuss these.

One of the critical decisions chain management needs to make is whether to have consistent hours across the chain or different store hours by location.

Consistency versus optimization

The fundamental decision about standard chain-wide or location specific store hours is one of consistency and continuity versus optimization. There are advantages and disadvantages to each approach, and as you look at retailers in your market, you'll find plenty of examples of both. Let's briefly review some of these.

© TOTEM Building Supplies Ltd. 2003

Figure 2-10

Standardized chain-wide store hours

The key advantage of having standardized store hours is continuity and simplicity. In this case, continuity and simplicity applies to marketing communications and staff scheduling. With standardized store hours, every advertisement or communication can simply state the stores' hours without having the burden of describing the variations by location. This enables retailers to spend much less time and space (*i.e.* in print ads or flyers) on communicating store hours.

From a staff planning and scheduling perspective, it is far easier to manage staffing levels and costs across a number of locations if store hours are consistent. Variations in store hours by location, though manageable at the store-level, can get complicated when rolled up across all stores. Question: Why does store 22 have 10% higher labor costs? Answer: Because they're opened longer hours than the other stores. This could get confusing over a large number of stores.

From the customer's point of view, consistent hours mean they don't have to worry about knowing the hours by location. Customers have enough to think about—if they get to your store, that's a victory in itself! If for whatever reason on a particular day, a customer decides to visit a different location, they might be a little perturbed if they found the store closed because the store hours at that particular location were different from the store at which they normally shop.

Location-specific store hours

The key advantage of having location-specific store hours is that it provides a level of optimization that standardized hours simply cannot. For example, if you had a three-store chain and traffic distribution by location looked like the charts in Figures 2-11, 2-12, and 2-13—one back-end loaded, one normally distributed and one with a front-end distribution, the inefficiencies become clear.

In store #1, it might be beneficial to have later store hours, as traffic levels are very strong near closing. At store #3, traffic is very strong at opening. This might suggest that opening the store earlier might make more sense in this location. With standardized store hours, optimizing store #1 and store #3 would not be possible.

Communications also become more of a challenge with location-specific store hours. Think about all the places that retailers promote or communicate store hours—advertisements, catalogs, signs, direct mail, websites, and more. Now multiply all these different

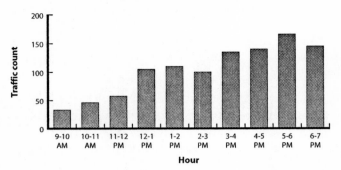

Figure 2-11

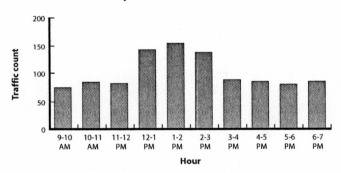

Figure 2-12

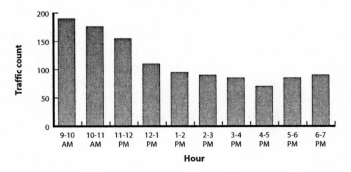

Figure 2-13

communications by the number of locations—it gets messy, doesn't it? But that's exactly what retailers who have location specific store hours manage.

Table 2-2

Store hours by location

Day(s)	Location #1	Location #2	Location #3
Mon/Tues	8 AM to 6 PM	8 AM to 6 PM	8 AM to 6 PM
Wed to Fri	8 AM to 9 PM	8 AM to 9 PM	8 AM to 9 PM
Saturday	9 AM to 5 PM	9 AM to 5 PM	9 AM to 5 PM
Sunday	11 AM to 5 PM	Noon to 5 PM	Noon to 5 PM

Day(s)	Location #4	Location #5	Location #6
Mon/Tues	8 AM to 5 PM	9 AM to 5 PM	9 AM to 5 PM
Wed to Fri	8 AM to 9 PM	8 AM to 9 PM	9 AM to 9 PM
Saturday	9 AM to 5 PM	9 AM to 5 PM	9 AM to 5 PM
Sunday	Noon to 5 PM	11 AM to 6 PM	11 AM to 6 PM

Day(s)	Location #7	Location #8	Location #9
Mon/Tues	9 AM to 6 PM	8 AM to 6 PM	8 AM to 6 PM
Wed to Fri	9 AM to 9 PM	8 AM to 9 PM	8 AM to 9 PM
Saturday	9 AM to 6 PM	9 AM to 5 PM	9 AM to 6 PM
Sunday	11 AM to 5 PM	Noon to 5 PM	11 AM to 6 PM

Although it might make perfect sense, and actually be even better for the business and customers to have location-specific store hours, it does create a level of complexity that should be understood.

There is no right way to set stores hours across multi-location retail chains. As this section has illustrated, there are both advantages and disadvantages to either method. The important point is that management think about these factors and formulate a store hour strategy that ultimately drives the best sales result, while balancing customer service, impact on staff, and overall expenses.

Chapter Summary

- There are no hard and fast rules to setting and refining store hours. Deciding what your store operating hours will be is a fundamental, yet tricky, decision that has many retailers second guessing themselves.

- There are a number of inputs retailers consider in establishing what their store hours should be, including customer feedback, competitors' hours, and business seasonality. Depending upon where the retail store is physically located, it may be subject to covenants that prescribe what the operating hours must be. Also, holidays and special events may compel retailers to modify store hours in order to maximize the sales opportunity.

- Traffic analysis is an extremely useful input into setting and refining store hours. Daily traffic distribution, or traffic by hour, can vary. These inter-day patterns usually fall into one of three general categories: front-end loaded, back-end loaded or normally distributed. By understanding these hourly traffic patterns, retailers will be able to identify opportunities to optimize store hours to better match traffic patterns.

- Extending store hours during special events, holidays or different seasons is common in retail. The underlying assumption in extending store hours is that incremental operating hours will lead to incremental traffic and consequently incremental sales? Unfortunately this isn't always the case. By analyzing traffic data, retailers can understand exactly what happens when they extend store hours—sometimes traffic merely shifts and total traffic does not increase. This can lead to higher staff expenses for little or no additional sales revenue.

- There are a number of consequences to changing store hours that retailers need to consider, including the cost and effort of communicating the new hours, the cost of staffing the additional hours, potential "wear-and-tear" on staff, and customer confusion.

- In multi-location retail chains, the challenge of setting and refining store hours takes on added complexity. Ultimately, chains need to decide whether they will employ standardized store hours across the entire chain or employ location-specific hours. Though there is no one right or wrong answer to this, there are advantages and disadvantages to each.

- Standardized store hours across a chain are less confusing and easier to communicate to customers, and they simplify staff scheduling. The downside is that standard operating hours may not be optimal for all locations equally. With location-specific operating hours, store hours can match the unique traffic patterns more precisely for each store, potentially resulting in higher levels of customer service and total sales. The downside is that communicating different store hours for numerous locations can be unruly from a communications standpoint and potentially confusing to customers.

The Impact of Weather on Traffic

You can't control the weather,
but you can control what you do
when weather happens.

The Impact of Weather on Traffic

IN MANY WAYS THE WEATHER and traffic are kindred spirits. Like weather, traffic is somewhat unpredictable and constantly changing. Although the science of meteorology and the technology meteorologists use to forecast the weather has advanced significantly, forecasts are still only forecasts.

Like the many factors that can influence retail traffic patterns, weather is no different. In this case, management can really claim they have no control over this one! What happens to traffic when a major snow storm hits? What happens when the weather is sunny and warmer than normal? Heavy rain? Extreme cold?

THE WEATHER
- Traffic and weather
- Store characteristics and the weather
- Managing the weather

Weather forecasting has evolved and the availability of weather information and forecasts has increased significantly over the years. With this greater availability, retail managers have a potentially powerful tool at their disposal. Of course, weather forecasts aren't always right, but they have never been better. If a retail manager has an understanding of how different types of weather have impacted his store's traffic patterns historically, then he will be able to make an educated guess at what might happen the very next time that particular weather occurs.

In this chapter we will explore the different ways weather can impact retail traffic. It may not be exactly what you thought. In addition to describing the impact on traffic patterns, we'll also discuss how managers can make the most of weather—even inclement weather.

Traffic patterns and weather

Naturally the type of weather conditions that impact retail traffic will depend upon what typical or normal conditions are for a particular geographic area. Obviously, the kind of weather that will impact retail traffic in Buffalo will be different in Miami.

The key is for retail managers to understand specifically what types of weather conditions or events affect his or her store. In order to do this effectively, retail managers need to stay on top of weather forecasts and consider how those forecasts might impact traffic in their store based on historical patterns.

When we consider the impact that weather can have on retail traffic patterns, it is helpful to think of the weather impact as a positive response (traffic increases), a negative response (traffic decreases) or neutral (traffic patterns are unaffected).

Weather conditions can have a positive impact on traffic, a negative impact or no impact. Bad weather can impact traffic in different

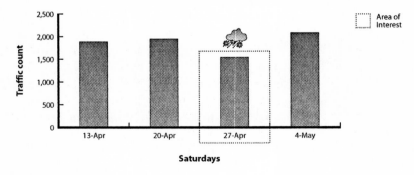

Figure 3-1

ways. For example, the chart in Figure 3-1 shows the traffic levels by day for a range of Saturdays for a particular retailer. On April 27, there was a material weather event and, as the chart shows, the traffic response was negative—that is, traffic dropped by 22%.

In the next example of an inclement day shown in Figure 3-2, bad weather actually resulted in a positive traffic response for this retailer—traffic actually went up by 17% compared to the non-inclement Saturdays.

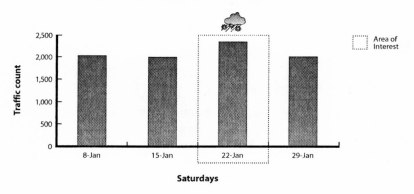

Figure 3-2

We'll now look at some examples of more specific traffic responses to various weather conditions—both positive and negative.

Precipitation

Generally, any type of weather that impacts prospects' mobility will have a negative impact on traffic. As one might expect, snow, especially snow storms with blowing snow that create poor visibility, have a significant impact on traffic. Snow that accumulates on the streets and walkways tend to have the most negative traffic response. Although any type of precipitation can negatively impact traffic, the more severe the precipitation, the more negative the traffic response will be, as illustrated in Figure 3-3.

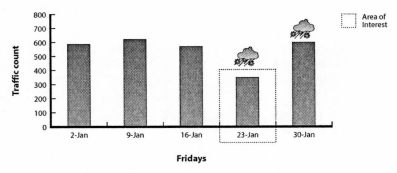

Figure 3-3

Negative traffic response

Weather can have a significant impact on traffic volumes. The chart in Figure 3-4 below shows traffic volumes by day for the month of January. From January 2 through January 24, average daily traffic volumes were approximately 11,300 counts. From January 25 through January 30, the region was hit by a strong blast of winter weather. Temperatures dropped significantly below seasonal averages and there were large accumulations of snow. As the chart

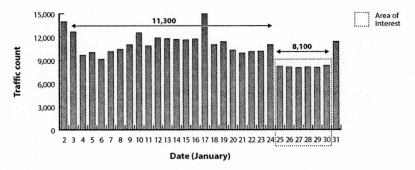

Figure 3-4

shows, the average daily traffic during this period was just over 8,100 counts—that's 28% below the daily average prior to the inclement weather! Once the weather returned to normal, traffic increased—but only back to seasonal average levels, which means some traffic was lost.

Positive traffic response

Inclement weather does not always create a negative traffic response. In fact, bad weather can actually create a positive traffic response for some retailers. In the chart below, a nasty winter storm rolled into the area, bringing with it freezing rain and treacherous driving conditions. As the chart in Figure 3-5 shows, the retail traffic response in this retail location was actually positive! How can this be possible? Freezing rain significantly and negatively impedes mobility—how can the traffic response be positive?

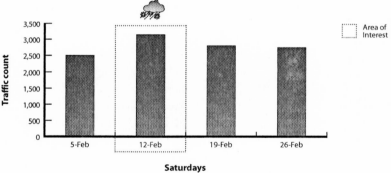

Figure 3-5

Although it is instructive to generalize about traffic responses to weather, as previously mentioned, traffic response will vary based on a number of factors including product offering, store location, and other site characteristics which we will now examine in more detail.

Oh, and as for this example where the positive traffic response seems counterintuitive—what do you want to bet that this particular retailer sells bags of ice salt, snow shovels and various other items that are extremely popular and almost necessities for making walkways and driveways safe in freezing rain conditions?

Store characteristics and weather impact

Although we can generalize how different types of weather events may impact traffic patterns, in order to understand how weather might impact your store, we need to first understand more about your location. Weather impacts different types of retailers in different ways—bad weather for some retailers can drive traffic up; for other retailers good weather can drive traffic down.

Product Offering—selling umbrellas on a rainy day

Fundamentally, traffic response as it relates to weather will be directly affected by what you sell. If what you sell is what people desperately need, regardless of the weather, your traffic may remain relatively unaffected. To the extent that your customers can defer their purchase to another day (*i.e.* when the weather gets better), your traffic will be impacted to some extent. Clearly what you sell will affect how weather affects traffic in your store. Let's look at the two broad categories: necessities and deferrable purchases.

Necessities

Regardless of the weather, if customers need what you offer, traffic may be relatively unaffected by weather conditions. That said, it is important to keep in mind that almost any purchase can be deferred—at least over the very short-term. For example, generally, people cannot defer grocery shopping for an extended period of time; regardless of how inclement the weather is, people will still need to buy food. If the weather is really bad, you might decide to dig a little deeper in the pantry to find something that could work and hold off on grocery shopping until the next day or even the day after, but if you have a baby in the house and you are out of baby formula or diapers, it won't matter how inclement the weather is, Mom or Dad will make the shopping trip—they have no choice. And of course, in the case of extreme weather events like hurricanes, for example, retail traffic in hardware and grocery stores can spike dramatically as people clamor to stock up on survival items.

Deferrable purchases

As mentioned, almost any purchase can be deferred, but some purchases are more deferrable than others. Retailers who sell products like automobiles, furniture or consumer electronics for example, tend to see significantly more negative traffic responses to inclement weather. It just makes sense. Who in their right mind is going to risk life and limb to travel out in a blizzard to check out the latest in home theatres or to have a peak at the new model sports sedan at their local dealership? The reality is that a few brave souls still will venture out, but many more won't. The challenge facing retail management is to predict how many—quantifying the expected traffic response. However, just before we tackle this issue, let's review how physical site characteristics can also affect traffic response.

Physical location characteristics

In addition to the types of products a retailer offers, a number of physical site characteristics can influence the traffic response to weather—both positively and negatively. Given that precipitation is a key variable in traffic response, location and accessibility need to be considered.

Mall locations

Although extreme weather can influence any type of retailer, malls tend to be affected in different ways. Inclement weather with precipitation can actually increase traffic as customers flock to malls to get out of the elements. Furthermore, mall shopping enables prospects to visit many retailers all under one roof. Interestingly, mall traffic can also be driven up when the weather gets extremely warm as people flock to the comfort of air conditioned malls to get a respite from the heat.

Freestanding destination locations

The proximity to parking and the distance from the parking lot to the store entrance will influence the traffic response to inclement weather. Naturally, if customers have a long walk or if there are any other factors that might mean that customers are more exposed to the elements, then traffic may be negatively affected.

City center locations

Inclement weather tends to impact free-standing suburban locations more than stores located in city center locations. This is intuitive as prospects traveling to a city center offices are already forced to travel to the area anyway.

The charts in Figures 3-6 and 3-7 show the traffic responses at two stores from the same chain in the same market. Store A is located

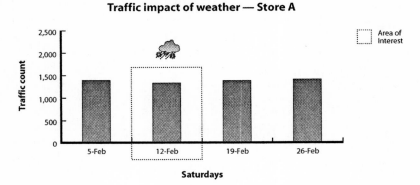

Figure 3-6

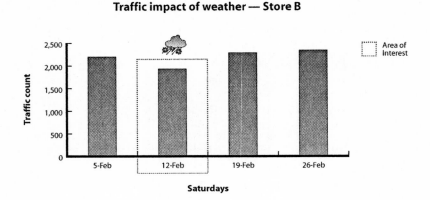

Figure 3-7

in the city's downtown core, while store B is located in a suburban power center. As the charts show, the traffic response to the inclement weather at store A is significantly less than store B. Specifically, store A received traffic levels only 5% off the average daily traffic for the period, while store B was off 15% from the average.

Travel distance and vehicular traffic

The travel distance required getting to your shopping destination and the complexity of the trip will impact the traffic response to a weather event. For example, driving around in a major city like Chicago in bad weather is a considerably more daunting task than driving in a smaller city like Peoria. If you are a furniture retailer located off a major freeway in Chicago, naturally you would expect a more negative traffic response than a suburban location that does not require travel on a major freeway.

Weather and seasonality

In a way, the changing of seasons is just another weather change. While we tend to think of weather events in the short-term (*i.e.* the current conditions), a change in season is essentially a larger change in the prevailing weather for a specific geographic area.

Naturally weather changes over the seasons—and so does retail traffic in your store. Good and bad weather is relative to the season. Bad weather in the summer might be a major rain storm;

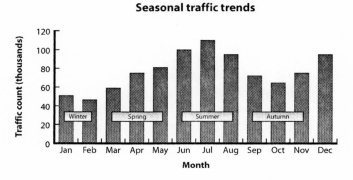

Figure 3-8

bad weather in the winter might mean freezing temperatures and a blizzard.

In order to manage the impact of the weather, retailers need to understand not only how their traffic changes based on short-term or extreme weather conditions, but also how it changes over the seasons. Traffic patterns over the seasons might look like the example in Figure 3-8.

Managing the weather

Of course there really is no way to "manage" the weather—that said, by knowing what the likely traffic response to various weather conditions and weather events in your store, you will be in a position to guess a lot better than you might have otherwise. There is no question that weather will impact traffic—the management challenge is to try to estimate what the impact will be and then undertake store-level strategies that benefit the business.

The key to this is to make sure you have enough data points to make an educated guess. If you really only consider what happened the last time a particular weather event occurred (assuming you can actually remember), you may guess wrong.

In this section we will discuss specifically how managers can use weather and traffic information to optimize performance and reduce costs.

Statistical weather modeling and other rocket science

The statisticians reading this book might say that in order to accurately and precisely understand the traffic response to weather, formal statistical techniques need to be employed. This may indeed be true, and in fact, with enough traffic and weather data you could actually use statistical models to calculate probabilities on the impact of weather; however, like meteorologists who employ very sophisticated models and techniques for forecasting the weather, no matter how sophisticated the models, they are not always right. Retail managers have a lot to manage—doing complex traffic modeling based on weather forecasts is likely not something a typical retail manager is trained to do or should spend time doing—hey, you have a store to run here!

Management tactics

Although most retailers intuitively understand that weather can impact business, it can be onerous to track, measure and recall previous weather events and the corresponding impact on traffic. The extent of management focus on weather is usually minimal if it exists at all. For example, you might overhear a manager saying, "The last time we got hit by a snow storm like the one they're forecasting, the store was dead." Hardly a rigorous analysis, though directionally correct. And, that's the point. Being *directionally* correct is really all a manager can hope to be. Moreover, being directionally correct can be a very powerful tool in helping make the most of what Mother Nature throws at you.

Specifically, here is what retail managers should do in order to manage the impact of weather in their store more effectively—to make the most out of the weather:

1. Monitor traffic

In order to have any hope of managing the impact of weather, managers need to track traffic. Without a baseline of traffic patterns, it's impossible to measure what the impact will likely be. It's not good enough to say, "last time we had a snow storm like this the store was dead." The key problem with this type of weather assessment is that although it may be directionally correct, it relies on human recollection—which is never very reliable—and it's not quantifiable. What does "dead" mean? Was traffic down by 50%? 25%? Or something else?

2. Review previous traffic patterns

The only way a manager will be able to practically make decisions about the weather with traffic data is if she can quantify the likely impact. Assuming the retailer has been tracking traffic over an extended period, the first step is simply to review what happened to traffic during similar weather events in the past. For example, the chart in Figure 3-9 shows a series of days where a significant snowfall occurred. By comparing these snowfall days to average traffic volumes for these days shows that the traffic response ranged from a decrease of 15% to 25%. Now the manager has something to work with—I guess "dead" means a 15% to 25% decrease in traffic!

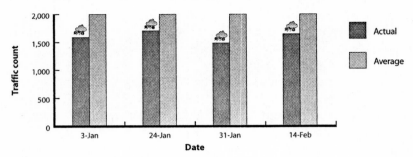

Comparison of weather events to average traffic volumes

Figure 3-9

By understanding what has happened in the past, management will have a good idea of what might happen to traffic when similar weather is forecast and can start to quantify the impact.

3. Review staffing levels and adjust

Staffing is usually the first place to start in deciding what to do about weather. Depending on the retailer, a manager might decide to reduce staffing in anticipation of a decrease in traffic as a result of expected weather. In this case, if a manager expects a 20% decrease in traffic, he might adjust staffing levels by this amount. That said, because weather is unpredictable, the manager would be well advised to be more conservative in their staff reduction because you can never tell exactly how traffic might be affected. For example, the manager might conservatively decrease staffing by only 10%—this would deliver an expense reduction to the company, but also provide enough staffing in the event that the traffic response is not as significant as expected. If the manager cuts too aggressively, say 25% of staff, and traffic levels were only modestly impacted or (hard to imagine) the weather forecast was not correct and the store traffic was either normal or above normal, this decision could hurt the business as frustrated prospects walk out because of long lines at tills or because they can't find a salesperson.

4. Other "non-customer" activities

The answer is not always to look at reducing staff. As mentioned, the weather and the resulting traffic response cannot be estimated with complete certainty. However, if historical traffic patterns show that traffic will likely drop given a particular expected weather event, there's a good chance it will again—but it might not. Can you afford the risk? Some managers just don't feel comfortable reducing staff or, because of company policy and/or expectations on the part of employees of getting a minimum number of working hours in a week, they simply cannot alter staffing levels.

In these situations, there are other ways managers can use traffic and weather information to their advantage. In retail, customers come first, or that's how it should be—however, there always seems to be more to do than there is time in the day. When the weather turns bad and the result is decreased prospect traffic, this is an excellent opportunity to start tackling those countless tasks that are important but there never seems time for. Two classic areas are merchandising and training.

- **Merchandising**

  Even in stores that are impeccably merchandised, there is always something to do. Major changes to plan-o-grams and store layouts can require a significant effort. Whether it's a total re-set of a particular department or just a modest clean-up, taking advantage of reduced prospect traffic to merchandise the store is a great use of the time. If a manager is expecting a decrease in traffic during the upcoming weekend based on a weather forecast, she can create a merchandising "to do" list in advance of the weather event. If the weekend comes and the weather forecast was wrong, no problem—it's business as usual. If the traffic response is materially negative, she will be ready to get staff working on merchandising right away.

- **Training**

  Whether it's learning about company policies, new systems, products or good old-fashioned sales techniques, training is always a challenge to schedule and deliver at the store-level. Like merchandising, inclement weather that results in a negative traffic response provides an excellent opportunity to conduct training. The key is to plan ahead and be flexible. Once the manager has estimated what the traffic response might be to the forecast weather event, she should then devise a mini-plan that balances training requirements with service levels. For example, it would not be prudent for a manager to plan an "all hands" training session based on weather. However, the manager could organize a short training session in such a way that if more prospects visit the store than was expected, the team would be ready to jump back into action.

Inclement weather that negatively impacts prospect traffic is not always a bad thing. As this section shows, sometimes this type of weather is really a great opportunity for managers to get ahead by knocking off some of those things that they never have time to do. These activities might not improve sales on the day of a major snowstorm, but it will prepare the store and staff to be even more effective when the weather gets better—and that will positively impact the business in the long-run.

Chapter Summary

- You can't control the weather but you certainly can control what you do when weather happens.

- The traffic response to weather can be negative (*i.e.* traffic drops compared to average levels), it can be positive (*i.e.* traffic increases compared to average traffic levels) or it can be neutral *(i.e.* there is no impact on traffic patterns).

- One of the key determinants to traffic response is precipitation, and more specifically, precipitation that negatively impacts prospect mobility.

- In addition to precipitation, there are numerous location-specific factors that will affect the traffic response to weather including product offering and the physical characteristics of the location.

- Product offering also plays a role in traffic response. When the products offered are necessities (*e.g.* food, medicine, *etc.*) traffic will be less affected than for retailers who offer products that are not necessities.

- Physical location characteristics such as mall versus non-mall, city center versus suburban, travel distance and market size (*i.e.* large city versus small town) can all influence the traffic response to weather and need to be considered on a location-by-location basis.

- The changing seasons represent changes to the prevailing weather patterns for a particular geographic region. Managers should be aware of how the changing seasons impact traffic.

- Although managers can employ more robust statistical methods to develop a higher level of precision in modeling the traffic response to a given weather pattern or event, it is likely not practical or necessary for a manager to do this. By reviewing previous traffic patterns compared to weather events, managers can get a good idea of what will likely happen—at least directionally. By looking at the traffic and weather data in a little more detail, they can quickly develop a quantitative estimate of what the traffic response will be. With this estimate in hand, the manager can either make a staffing adjustment (*i.e.* staff up or down in anticipation of the traffic response) or plan to do other "non-customer" activities such as merchandising or training.

CHAPTER

Sales Conversion
Turning shoppers into buyers

"Conversion rate is to retail what batting average is to baseball—without knowing it, you can say somebody had a hundred hits last season, but you don't know whether he had three hundred at-bats or a thousand."
– Paco Underhill,
Why We Buy: The Science of Shopping

Sales Conversion

WHEN YOU ASK A RETAILER the one very basic question every retailer MUST know the answer to—"Of the total number of prospects that visit your store, how many actually buy?"—the reaction you get is very interesting. First, the retailer looks at you like you've just asked him the most obvious question in the world—kind of like, "What's your favorite color?" Then, as he starts to formulate his response, you can see the gears starting to turn—"OK, OK I know I've seen this on a management report somewhere... Hum... what's that damn number..." A few seconds (or minutes) later, panic strikes. In that moment he realizes that he doesn't know the answer. So like any good manager he takes a wild guess— but he says it with authority so that it sounds indisputable—"a very large percentage actually buys" or (I love this one) "industry stats say it's about 25%." Of course such statistics don't really exist. Busted!

SALES CONVERSION

• Conversion defined

• No traffic, no conversion

• Sales vs. conversion

• Calculating conversion rates

• Conversion and traffic

• Factors affecting conversion

• Driving conversion rates

Whether you sell cars or cameras, shoes or shovels, and everything in between, you actually do have a sales conversion rate—you just don't know it (yet). Sales conversion rates, like the weather, are constantly changing. So, like the weather, you need to check the temperature frequently and continually. However, unlike the weather, you can actually influence sales conversion rates in your store.

In this chapter we will explore sales conversion in great depth. It is the most fundamental and critical concept that a retailer—all retailers—must understand.

Sales conversion defined

To ensure an accurate calculation of sales conversion rates, we need to start with a mathematical basis or formula. The sales conversion formula is as follows:

$$\frac{\Sigma = .5\Pi(3.75y^2) \cong Z}{a + b + c}$$

Stop! Don't shut the book—I'm kidding. If the formula for calculating sales conversion rates really was this difficult, no retailer on the face of the planet would be able to calculate it! (Myself included.)

Actually, sales conversion is calculated very simply, as follows:

$$\text{Sales Conversion} = \frac{\text{Sales Transactions}}{\text{Traffic}}$$

For example, if on a particular day, your store did 500 transactions (or individual sales) and the total prospect traffic in your store during the day was 1,000, then your sales conversion rate for the day would be 0.5 or 50% (500/1000=0.5). Pretty simple.

No traffic, no conversion

"Transactions" are defined as unique sales, that is, a person who comes to the till with one or several items to buy. Virtually every retailer can tell you, without even a moment's hesitation, precisely how many transactions or sales they have made in a day. Furthermore, retailers have sliced and diced these transaction numbers, plotted charts and graphs of them; they can even quote year-over-year comparatives, average number of items per transaction and average sale amounts. Are you kidding, every retailer worth her salt can tell you this! But, unfortunately, most can't tell you what their sales conversion rate is because they don't know their traffic count. As basic as the sales conversion formula is, without knowing your traffic count, you don't have a denominator and therefore can't complete the calculation.

It's not that I particularly take pleasure in making retailers feel uncomfortable by asking the "conversion rate" question, but when I visit a retailer's store and I don't see any traffic counting mechanism, I know they cannot calculate conversion rates—it's impossible without a traffic count. And if they don't know what their sales conversion rate is, then they don't fully understand how their business is performing. Period.

It's all about sales—right?

On numerous occasions I've been taken to task by retailers on the importance of sales conversion. They say, "I track sales—sales are everything. If sales are going up, I know I'm doing well." Well, it's not usually a long argument, because I agree—sales are important. But, if you look at sales alone to measure your performance, you are not getting the whole story. Here's why.

Let's say that on Day 1 a retailer had $31,500 in sales (based on 630 transactions) and on Day 2 sales jumped 40% to $44,100 (based on 882 transactions). You can see the impact in Figure 4-1. The average sale value was $50 on both days. Furthermore, let's assume that profitability is the same percentage of sales on both days. Great! Most retailers would be very pleased with this result—why wouldn't they?

OK, so far, so good. But here's some additional information to consider.

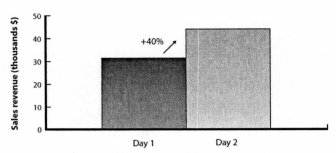

Figure 4-1

On Day 1, total customer traffic was 1,750 and 3,392 on Day 2. Of course, now that we have this information we can plug it into our new formula (the actual formula) to calculate sales conversion rates as shown below in Table 4-1.

Table 4-1

$$\text{Conversion Rate} = \frac{\text{Transactions}}{\text{Traffic}}$$

Day 1	Day 2
$.36 = \dfrac{630}{1{,}750}$	$.26 = \dfrac{882}{3{,}392}$

Although transactions, or sales, went up by 40% on Day 2, the sales conversion rate actually went down ten percentage points or by 28%. As one retailer so succinctly put it—"So what? Sales still went up. I don't get your point."

Here's the point. Although it is good that sales went up on Day 2, the fact is, it could have been a lot better. To be more precise, if, on Day 2, the retailer could have maintained a 36% conversion rate (instead of dropping to 26%), then 1,221 total transactions would have been made—or 591 additional sales. Assuming the average sale was worth $50 on both days, this would add up to an incremental $29,550 in sales. Think about it. If conversion rates could have been held at 36% on both days, and the average sale remained $50, then this retailer would have actually increased sales by 94% over Day 1! Magical, isn't it? Here's the math in Table 4-2 just to prove it:

Table 4-2

Performance vs. the sales opportunity

	Day 1	Day 2	
Conversion Rate	36% (Actual)	26% (Actual)	36% (Target)
Traffic	1,750	3,392	3,392
Transactions	630	882	1,221
Average Sale	$50.00	$50.00	$50.00
Total Revenue	**$31,500**	**$44,096**	**$61,056**

+ 40%

+ 94%

So, it's not that increasing sales isn't something to be happy about, but I'd be happier if I knew I was making the most of the opportunity. A 40% increase is nice, but a 94% increase is even nicer. I can only be unhappy with 40% if I know 94% was possible and I can only know that 94% was possible by knowing sales conversion rates.

Calculating conversion rates

Now that we've covered the general idea of sales conversion, let's start digging into some of the many nuances of calculating conversion rates. To accurately calculate conversion rates, you need to ensure that the variables in the sales conversion formula (*i.e.* number of transaction counts and traffic counts) are accurate. If you suspected that this conversion stuff is not quite as easy as it looks, you would be correct. But it's not rocket science either. Let's start by looking at traffic counts, and then we'll take on transaction counts.

Traffic counting methods

If a retailer is counting traffic (most don't even bother), there are several ways they can actually collect traffic counts. And, depending upon how the retailer is actually counting traffic, the count precision can vary significantly. The method you use to count traffic will impact conversion rates so lets take a moment to review the three general categories of traffic counting methods:

- **Electronic traffic counting devices**

  The most common electronic traffic equipment use infrared sensors at the store entrance to capture traffic counts and then transmit the data to a data collection device. The raw traffic data is then manipulated with reporting software. The downside to this technology is that it's not very smart. In other words, every time the electronic beam is broken (*i.e.* whenever anyone walks in or out through the door), a count is registered. There are more sophisticated video-capture and heat sensing solutions that can determine not only the traffic count but track the direction of the traffic (*i.e.* in or out) and even the general characteristics of the prospect entering the store (*i.e.* male or female). The downside to this technology is complexity and cost. These systems can be very expensive.

- **Mechanical turnstiles with "clicker" counters**

  Capturing traffic counts with turnstiles is a low-tech way of getting some basic traffic information, but it's not necessarily cheap (turnstiles can be expensive) or practical for capturing traffic data. For example, you literally need to read the count off of each turnstile, so if you have several of these it can be a pain. And most retailers don't have time to regularly jot the traffic numbers down, so if they get the count once a day they're probably lucky. If you want to look at traffic counts on an hourly basis, it's even more of a pain. Lastly, turnstiles are not especially customer friendly. Generally, in this high-tech day and age, customers don't like being herded through turn-stiles. Furthermore, in many types of retail formats, turnstiles just wouldn't be practical.

- **Manual counts by staff**

  Having staff manually count traffic can work in very low traffic volume scenarios, but it's still not especially practical. For example, it's not uncommon for a luxury auto dealer to have the receptionist count "ups." But during lunch breaks, or when the receptionist is distracted on the phone, counts get missed. Manual traffic counting is better than nothing, but not by much.

Refining the traffic count

In many ways, collecting the raw traffic data is the easy part. Refining the gross traffic count in order to determine the actual number of prospects that come into your store can be a challenge. Depending upon the retailer, there is always some level of traffic noise, that is, non-prospect traffic. Some retailers have a significant amount of non-prospect traffic while others have very little. Traffic noise can be caused by a number of factors, including:

1. customer movements,

2. buying group size, and

3. staff movements.

In our quest to refine our prospect counts, it is important to understand these causes.

- **Customer movements**

  Depending on the type of retailer, prospects may need to enter and exit the store (sometimes many times) as part of the shopping process. For example, auto dealers have among the highest percentage of non-prospect traffic, ranging from 85% to 98%—that's a lot of noise! It almost seems impossible, doesn't it? Here's a scenario to help put this in perspective.

Shopping for a vehicle

A husband and wife enter the showroom (2 counts registered), and they chat with a sales person who walks them out to the lot to show them a brand new Ford Explorer (3 more counts). After a brief discussion, they all come into the showroom to start negotiating (3 more counts registered). During the discussions, it's decided that the couple would really prefer the red SUV instead of the blue one, so, you guessed it, they all head back out to the lot (3 more counts), go for a test drive, and then come back into the showroom to finalize the deal (3 more counts). One last thing, to finalize the deal, the couple needs to show their current vehicle insurance documentation which is out in their old car—so the husband runs out to the car and back (2 more counts). Finally the new, happy SUV buyers leave the showroom (2 more counts). Of course, the salesperson walks them out to their car, and then comes back into the showroom to complete the paperwork (2 more counts).

In this case, the auto dealer is very progressive and is using a typical electronic traffic monitoring system.

I think you get the point. In this very plausible scenario, 20 gross traffic counts were registered. Being a sharp retailer, the gross traffic count is cut in half to account for the in/out counting (*i.e.* what comes in must go out, so to get a count of only incoming traffic you would divide the total count in half). That leaves us with 10 'in' counts. How many actual prospects were there in this example? One. Yes, one. Although the husband and wife are in fact two people, they are technically only one buyer. So the traffic noise would be 9 out of the 10 counts or 90%.

• Buying group size

As the previous example nicely demonstrates, there is not always (and rarely there is) a one-to-one relationship between traffic and prospects. Often people shop in groups—they're all not prospects. For example, entire families may visit a store together. Although all the family members may be possible buyers, at check out time they likely put all their purchases together for a single (albeit large) transaction. This would obviously understate the conversion rate. Buying group size can make it a challenge to get the precise number of prospects. As you will see later in this chapter, the work needed to refine the number may not be worth the effort.

- **Staff**

  It's not hard to imagine that staff alone (including delivery people, cleaning staff, etc.) can generate a significant amount of superfluous counts. Lunch breaks, helping customers carry their purchases to their vehicles, and shift changes all add up. The more staff you have, generally the more non-prospect traffic you will have.

Transaction counts

Most retailers have a point-of-sale (POS) system that can churn out transaction counts—some systems provide retailers transaction counts by the hour or even the minute! Of course, this will vary depending upon the type of retailer. For example, an exclusive jewelry store may only have a handful of transactions per day. Generally, determining transaction counts should be straight-forward for virtually any retailer. That said, retailers that have retail and non-retail transactions (for example, retail, corporate or Web sales) sometimes can have challenges with breaking out transaction types—of course we would only want to include retail traffic to calculate retail sales conversion. Also, some POS systems include product returns in the transaction counts. Although these are technically transactions, this isn't what we're measuring and they will need to be excluded.

Reliable data

No system is perfect, and occasionally anomalies in transaction or traffic counts can crop up. You need to watch for these and occasionally even modify or correct the data. For example, one retailer with an electronic traffic counting system nicely decorated their front entrance with garland for the Christmas season. A nice decorative touch, we thought. Unfortunately, the garland was only attached at the top of the door frame, allowing the ends of the garland to sway as the heat vents blew. These loose ends were blowing back and forth in front of their traffic monitoring sensors, generating thousands of counts! Boy, they had a pretty low conversion rate that day! The point is, stuff happens. You need to watch for days that seem way-off—there's a very good chance there are data issues.

Conversion rate precision

As you can see, calculating an absolutely precise conversion rate can be very difficult, if not impossible. Although it is easier to be more accurate in some retail formats than others (like in very low traffic/low transaction retailers for example), for most retailers, getting perfectly precise data is not practical. The good news is that retailers don't need absolutely precise numbers to get the critical insights that conversion rates can provide. In this section, we will describe a general framework for thinking about conversion rates and we will also discuss conversion rate granularity—what level of detail do you need?

All things being equal

Retailers often ask "How can I possibly calculate conversion rates when it's virtually impossible to get an accurate traffic count because there is so much non-customer traffic in my store?" In fact, this is likely why many retailers have not pursued conversion analysis sooner. When you have lots of staff coming and going, people shopping in buying groups and other factors already mentioned, it does seem insurmountable—well almost.

It is true that there can be a lot of noise in traffic data, but if the noise level is relatively consistent, it can be accounted for in the analysis. Here's an example:

A large technology retailer has 40 staff on the sales floor on any given day. Though the staff all come in from a special staff entrance, during the day, most of them will exit and re-enter from the main entrance numerous times—taking lunch breaks, helping customers carry purchases to their vehicles or simply to get some fresh air.

Over the course of the entire day, these staff counts can add-up to literally hundreds of non-customer counts.

Sound familiar? In this case, the retailer has two options for managing the traffic impact:

1. ignore the impact of staff counts or

2. estimate and eliminate the staff counts.

1. Ignore staff counts and focus on the percentages

If you assume that staff movements occur consistently, that is, on any given day these 40 staffers are going to be coming and going about the same number of times (which is very often the case), then you can ignore them and focus on conversion percentage increases and decreases or the conversion rate factor. For example, if the daily conversion rate (including all the staff noise in the traffic variable) is 50%, then this becomes the conversion rate factor or benchmark. Day in and day out, management should then focus on driving the conversion rate factor up – as long as the conversion rate factor stays at 50% or higher, management will know that they are holding their own from a conversion perspective.

As the chart in Figure 4-2 shows, even with the staff noise included, management has the ability to monitor conversion rates. Although data anomalies may come up, over time and with enough data

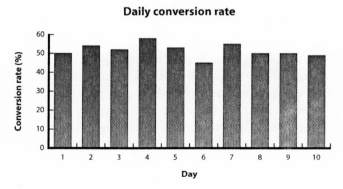

Figure 4-2

points, management will have a very good understanding of conversion rate changes. By including staff counts, the actual conversion rates will be understated because the traffic count is actually higher (*i.e.* because of staff) than the actual prospect count. The calculated conversion rate would be higher if you calculated the conversion rate based on the actual number of prospects (*i.e.* total traffic *less* staff counts). That all said, the important thing for management to monitor is how conversion rates are changing—either going up, staying flat or going down.

Table 4-3

Factoring out staff counts from the conversion rate

Description	
Daily gross traffic count including staff movements	2,000
Estimated movements of 40 staff during the day (assume staff generate 5 counts each per day)	200
Traffic excluding staff	1,800
Transaction count	1,000
Conversion Rate (excluding staff counts)	56%
Conversion Rate (including staff counts)	50%

2. Estimate and eliminate staff counts

In this approach management would estimate the staff impact on total counts, and then eliminate these staff counts from the total counts in order to more accurately estimate prospect traffic. In auto or furniture retailers, for example, where personal selling is a critical success factor, a more precise prospect count may be useful. Here's how the numbers might look if the computer store management decided to estimate and eliminate the staff counts:

As Table 4-3 shows, when staff counts are eliminated, the conversion rate increases. The staff elimination approach is not as problematic as it might have seemed at first. By simply adding up total staff numbers and estimating movements, management can develop quite an accurate estimate of the number of staff counts.

If more precision it desired, this can be accomplished through basic observation sampling. In other words, management would need to have staff count their movements for a day or two to get an estimate or have someone monitor staff, noting the total number of staff movements. Once a factor as been identified, this can be used on an on-going basis. Management might want to conduct periodic sampling just to be certain that the staff estimates haven't changed too much. It won't be perfect, but it will be close enough to provide management with a pretty good idea.

Conversion rate granularity—too much information!

The amount of granularity or level of detail that a retailer needs varies—one size does not fit all in this case. Some retailers can effectively use conversion rates by the hour; other retailers are better off looking at conversion on a weekly or even a monthly basis. The key here is using conversion rates effectively. There really is no point to going to all the effort of calculating conversion rates by the hour if you're only going to practically use daily conversion rates. Here are two ends of the spectrum to consider—most retailers will fall somewhere in between:

1. a large high volume mass consumer products retailer and

2. an auto dealer.

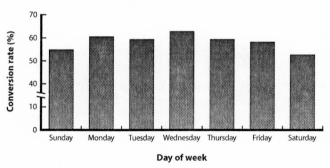

Figure 4-3

Example 1: Consumer products retailer

A high volume consumer products retailer is definitely interested in daily and even hourly conversion rates. As the chart in Figure 4-3 shows, there is variation in conversion rate by day-of-week and it is important for the retailer to understand the conversion rate patterns.

With an understanding of conversion rates by day, this retailer would also want to understand conversion rates by the hour of the day.

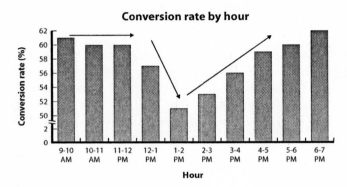

Figure 4-4

As the chart in Figure 4-4 shows, conversion rates can vary by the hour of the day. In this case, conversion rates dropped at 1 PM and then slowly tracked back up until closing. Upon further investigation it became clear that the conversion rates were decreasing because staff were taking lunch breaks from 1 PM to 3 PM. An understanding of these patterns can be very useful to management in this type of retail environment.

Example 2: Auto dealer

As described earlier, auto dealers have a significant amount of non-prospect traffic. And, by the very nature of how people shop for cars, the amount of movement in and out of the showroom is significant. This, along with the fact that comparatively speaking, auto dealers have relatively low transaction counts (*i.e.* a lot of traffic is generated—mostly noise—compared to the number of deals written or transactions on a given day) does strange things to conversion rates. Conversion rates by hour or even by day in this case, are not

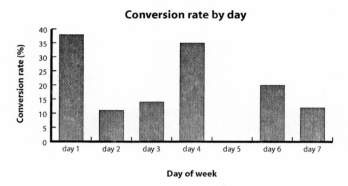

Figure 4-5

particularly meaningful to management. Interestingly, conversion rates become more meaningful in this type of retail environment when we look at them in aggregate on a weekly or monthly basis. As the chart in Figure 4-5 shows, conversion rates for auto dealers can swing dramatically from day to day. Although some of this can

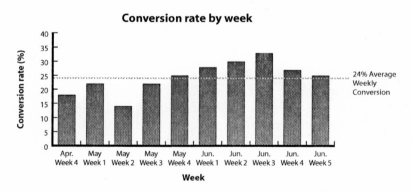

Figure 4-6

be explained by sales staff effectiveness, to a greater extent, it is a result of the noise in the traffic data.

Although looking at daily conversion rates may not be especially meaningful to auto dealers, conversion analysis becomes quite useful when we look at weekly and monthly averages. As the chart in Figure 4-6 shows, the conversion pattern becomes clearer when we look at more aggregated data.

When the data is REALLY noisy

When there is a lot of noise in the traffic data, it may be worth doing some basic observational surveying to estimate a prospect ratio. Again, auto dealers are a good example of this. To estimate a prospect ratio, simply have someone count actual prospects that come into the store over a period of time, compare these prospect counts to gross traffic counts for the same period and calculate the prospect ratio. Here's an example.

Prospect traffic in an auto dealer was monitored over several weeks during weekdays and weekends. This was done because the prospect counts were felt to be different on weekdays compared to weekends. This makes sense, as people tend to shop together as a family unit more on weekends than on weekdays.

As Table 4-4 shows, based on this sample during the weekday actual prospects made up only 4% of the gross traffic counts, while on the weekend the prospect traffic was 9% of the total traffic. In this case, prospect was defined as one buying group. So for example, a husband and wife may have come into the showroom together to shop for a vehicle, but they were counted as only one prospect. With the prospect ratios identified, we can now apply these ratios to total store traffic to calculate the estimated number of prospects that come into the dealership on any given day. Will these factors change? Yes, of course, they will change, but again consistency is the key. If the dealership consistently uses the same prospect ratios for weekdays and weekends, over time the conversion rates will be comparable and therefore provide management with a basis to gage relative conversion performance.

Conversion precision—final thoughts

Conversion rate precision is all about finding the level of detail that is appropriate for your needs—as you can see, it can vary significantly. When it comes to calculating conversion rates, precision

Table 4-4

Prospect count vs. gross traffic count

Weekday	Prospect Count	Traffic Count	Customer Ratio
9 to 10 AM	1	28	4%
10 to 11 AM	0	41	0%
11 to 12 PM	2	47	4%
12 to 1 PM	1	29	3%
1 to 2 PM	2	45	4%
2 to 3 PM	1	29	3%
3 to 4 PM	2	39	5%
4 to 5 PM	3	48	6%
Total	**12**	**306**	**4%**

Weekend	Prospect Count	Traffic Count	Customer Ratio
9 to 10 AM	3	40	8%
10 to 11 AM	4	51	8%
11 to 12 PM	5	55	9%
12 to 1 PM	5	62	8%
1 to 2 PM	6	70	9%
2 to 3 PM	7	75	9%
3 to 4 PM	5	60	8%
4 to 5 PM	5	54	9%
Total	**40**	**467**	**9%**

is nice, but it's not absolutely critical. Calculating conversion rates using a consistent basis is far more important.

Conversion rates and traffic patterns

OK, now that we've beaten sales conversion rate calculation to death, let's look at how conversion rates relate to traffic patterns. First, a quick review of terminology:

- **Customer** – a person who comes into your store and makes a purchase;
- **Non-buyer** – a person who visits your store, but doesn't make a purchase;
- **Traffic** – the total number of counts in your store; this includes customers, non-buyers and potentially non-customer traffic.

The reason it is important to be clear about these terms is that some retailers refer to their transaction count as their customer count. Strictly speaking this is correct; however, some retailers erroneously equate "customer count" with "traffic count." Clearly this is not the same thing. For example, 1,000 prospects may visit a store (traffic count), but only 500 of these may actually purchase something (customer count). When retailers tell me they know their customer

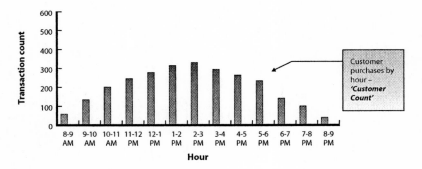

Figure 4-7

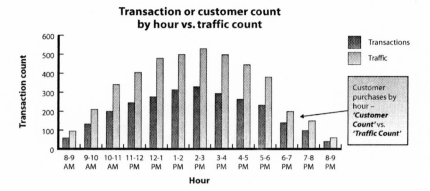

Figure 4-8

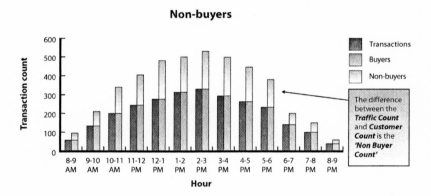

Figure 4-9

counts and therefore have no need to count the number of people who enter their store, I get nervous. Why? Because, managing 500 visitors is very different than managing 1,000 visitors. By saying your customer count is 500, you may be sub-optimizing (for example, under staffing) based on these actual buyers instead of focusing on the number of prospects—which may be a significantly higher number. The following charts in Figures 4-7, 4-8 and 4-9 provide a visual representation of the three categories of traffic counts.

So, let me get this straight: these non-buying prospects came to your store, wandered around, but didn't buy anything? Aren't you just a little curious about why?

Conversion is about the people who DON'T buy

Retailers are utterly obsessed with the number of customers who buy, or transactions. OK, I can understand this, but if you want to drive sales performance in your store, you need to focus on the prospects who DON'T buy! The customer who bought something must have been satisfied in some way; those that weren't satisfied obviously left without making a purchase. I'd want to know who these

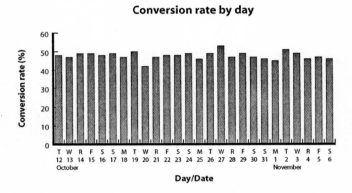

Figure 4-10

people are, how many of them there were, and most importantly, why they didn't buy.

In order to understand how many prospects you have, you need to start with the traffic counts—the volume and timing of the non-buyer traffic can tell you a lot about what you might need to do to turn more of these prospects into buyers. Let's start by looking at a range of conversion rates by day as illustrated in the chart in Figure 4-10.

For a moment, let's focus on the lowest conversion day (*i.e.* 42% on October 20th) and the highest conversion day (*i.e.* 53% on October 27th) which are highlighted in Figure 4-11. As it turns out, both of these days are Wednesdays. So, the question becomes, "What's

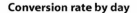

Conversion rate by day

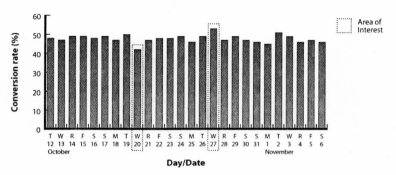

Figure 4-11

Conversion rate vs. traffic — Wednesdays

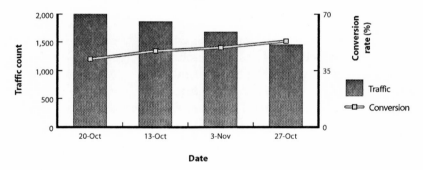

Figure 4-12

different about these two Wednesdays?" This is where the traffic data comes in.

The chart in Figure 4-12 shows conversion rates compared to traffic volume for the four Wednesdays in the data sample. Interestingly, when traffic volume is high (*i.e.* 2,000 counts on October 20th) the conversion rate is at its lowest—42%. As traffic volume progressively decreases, conversion rates progressively increase.

On the lowest traffic day only 1,450 prospect counts were registered, but the conversion rate jumped to 53%. Do you get the feeling that traffic volume and conversion rate are related?

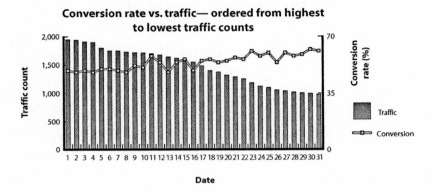

Figure 4-13

In order to see the broader relationship between traffic volume and conversion rates, we plotted the entire data sample of traffic volumes and conversion rates in the chart in Figure 4-13. As you can see, as traffic volumes increase, conversion rates generally tend to decrease. The opposite also holds true—when traffic volume decreases, conversion rates tend to increase. To be even more precise, you would want to compare similar days of the week. For example, the next step in this analysis would be to compare Mondays to Mondays, Saturdays to Saturdays, and so on.

With an understanding of the relationship between traffic and conversion rates, retailers are able to identify potential opportunities to drive overall sales performance. Now that we know that traffic and conversion rates are related, we'll turn our attention to the other factors that can influence conversion rates.

Factors that influence conversion rates

Almost without fail, once retailers discover the significance of conversion rates, their attention very quickly turns to influencing conversion. As one retailer put it, "OK, so now I know my conversion rate—what can I do about it?" This is, of course, the important question. The answer, however, is that there is no one right answer. Every retailer is different and every store (even stores in the same chain and same market) have different characteristics. While only you will know what the answer is for your store, let's review some of the key conversion drivers.

Sales staff effectiveness

For retailers who sell high involvement, expensive or complex products, personal selling is probably the key driver in sales conversion. Think of automobiles, jewelry, home entertainment products—all pretty good examples where personal selling is a significant factor in whether a prospect gets converted into a customer. Invariably, this comes down to a discussion about the characteristics that make for a good, or even great, salesperson. Here are a few things to consider:

- **Product Knowledge**

   There's nothing worse than rearranging your life to make time to visit a store that has something you're interested in buying, only to find yourself talking to a salesperson who knows a lot less about the product than you do. I realize that product knowledge is Sales 101, but you would be surprised at how often this can happen. If personal selling is important to your business, make sure you provide your sales staff with the time and tools to learn the product at a level necessary to make the sale. If you provide the time and tools, but some sales staff don't use them, get new sales staff.

- **Sales Training**

   Beyond a solid understanding of the products you carry (which is an absolute minimum), good salespeople also have a good understanding of selling. There are techniques and strategies to being a good salesperson—very few people are naturals. But the good news is that these techniques can be taught.

- **Appearance and professionalism**

   If product knowledge is Sales 101, then appearance and professionalism are Sales 100. As you will learn in any sales training, looks count. Again, it never ceases to amaze me how many retailers apparently tolerate sloppy appearance. Professional salespeople never look like they just rolled out of bed. Although it is a fine line between personal style and appropriateness, most retail managers know what's right for their store—don't be shy about communicating it to your salespeople.

• **Compensation plan**

Of course, there is no one right compensation plan; every retailer is truly different in this regard. The point here, however, is that if you want to drive conversion rates, you need to make sure your compensation plan encourages conversion. All the elements of the compensation plan like commission versus salary, bonus levels, targets and stretch targets need to reconcile with your sales objectives. A conversion rate target should be included in your list.

Staff levels

Just having the right number of staff in your store can significantly impact conversion rates. For example, if you are a large general merchandise retailer, you will want to make sure your staff schedules are mapped to traffic levels so that you can ensure you have proper coverage (more on this in *Chapter 5*). Especially in big box stores, you would be surprised how many prospects don't buy, not because the store didn't have what they wanted or even the right price, but simply because they couldn't find it!

Merchandising

Good merchandising is all about making products easy to find and buy. The more effective your merchandising, the more easily prospects will find what they're looking for. Again, this is especially critical in large format stores where thousands of prospects may visit during the day. In this case, the product displays will have to do a certain amount of the selling. Disheveled displayers, mixed up product and general disorganization gets in the way of a sale. If the prospect needs to track down a staffer to find a product, the probability of losing the sale goes up (*i.e.* they might not find a staffer). Furthermore, really effective merchandising may mean you don't need as many staff!

Till availability

How many times have you dashed into the mega-store and loaded up your arms with those odds and ends you needed, only to discover that the line-up at the till is the length of a football field! To add insult to injury, the mega-store has 22 check-out lanes, but only three are open! Retailers have been trying to solve the till availability problem for a long time—and some are actually pretty good at it. But many retailers still look only at customer or transaction counts to determine till staffing needs. Remember, this only tells them how many made it through the till, not how many who left because the lines were too long!

Promotional strategy

There's no question about it, hot deals will drive up conversion rates. Loss leaders, door crashes or other one-of-a-kind buys will drive up conversion rates as customers stream into your store to take advantage of the great offer. Unfortunately, these deals don't always drive conversion rates up as high as retailers would like. Also, these hot deals are usually made possible by slashing margins—you may generate more sales, but it's rarely profitable. Of course, the hope is that customers buy some other products to go along with the hot deal or sale item.

Product mix, availability and price

You need to have what people want, when they want it, at a price they're willing to pay. It is what retail lives (and dies) for. Obviously, stock-outs will hurt conversion rates—it's not hard to understand why.

Buying group size

Although buying group has been mentioned previously, it is important to understand that buying group size will impact conversion rates. Here's how. Depending on the type of retailer, people may shop alone or in groups. For example, furniture shopping is often done with a spouse or other family members. Although sometimes people will shop alone, more frequently it is in a group. On the other hand, shopping for personal items—shoes, cosmetics or books—is more often done in buying groups of one.

There isn't really anything a retailer can do to encourage or discourage buying group size. More than anything it's just important to understand what the buying group size is and factor it into the conversion rate calculation. It is important to realize, however, that buying group sizes can change over the course of a week. For example, buying groups tend to be larger on the weekends than weekdays, as one would expect. As a result, it follows that conversion rates will likely be lower on a Saturday than a Wednesday.

Competitive environment

Consumers have choice. Often, lots of choice. If your competitor is having a grand opening or some other major sales event, this could naturally impact your conversion rates—at least temporarily. Again, retailers, by and large, are already keenly aware of their competitors and what they are up to. It is not something you can actually control, but it is important to understand it. The fact is, competitors' activities can affect your traffic levels, and potentially, conversion rates.

Conversion factors summary

One of the great challenges retail managers face is in trying to identify the biggest sales conversion levers for their stores—which may be any one or a combination of some of the factors just discussed. Once the manager identifies the key conversion factors, she needs to formulate strategies and execute against these strategies in an effort to positively affect conversion rates. Most retailers already have an intuitive sense about what will drive conversion in their stores—there rarely is a "knock-out" punch or obvious tactic that hadn't been considered at some point. The difference is, now with a way to actually measure conversion rates, managers can begin to experiment—implement a program and see if conversion rates change. It's OK to experiment now that you have a way to measure. Here's a list of the conversion factors again for your reference:

- Sales staff effectiveness
- Staffing levels
- Merchandising
- Till availability

- Promotional strategy
- Product mix, availability and price
- Buying group size
- Competitive environment

Driving sales performance with conversion rates

Conversion rate is one of the most critical retail performance metrics—if not the most important. By consistently tracking conversion rates and refining processes that drive the biggest conversion levers, retail managers can drive significant sales performance gains in their stores. But, as I'm sure some of the readers have already figured out, conversion rates alone will not win the game.

Retail sales performance equation

The following equation identifies the three key variables that generate the sales result:

$$\textbf{Sales Revenue} = \textbf{Traffic} \times \textbf{Conversion} \times \frac{\textbf{Average}}{\textbf{Sale Value}}$$

According to the formula, sales revenue is a function of three variables: traffic volume (TRAFFIC), sales conversion rate (CONVERSION) and average sale value (AVERAGE SALE). Here's an example to illustrate the point. In order to generate $50,000 in sales, this retailer had to convert 50% of the 1,000 prospects who visited her store and had an average sale value of $100.

$$\textbf{\$50,000} = \textbf{1,000} \times \textbf{50\%} \times \textbf{\$100}$$

If this retailer wants to drive sales performance up to $75,000, there are a number of different ways this can be achieved:

1. Increase traffic volume

If the retailer were able to drive traffic volume up by 50% to 1,500 prospects (*i.e.* through increased advertising or promotions) and at the same time was able to maintain a 50% conversion rate and $100 average sale, then she would achieve $75,000 in sales.

$$\$75,000 = \boxed{1,500} \times 50\% \times \$100$$

2. Increase conversion rate

If the retailer were able to drive her conversion rate up to 75% (*e.g.* through sales training) even if prospect traffic remained constant at 1,000 and average sale at $100, then she could achieve $75,000 in sales.

$$\$75,000 = 1,000 \times \boxed{75\%} \times \$100$$

3. Increase average sale

If the retailer were able to increase her average sale from $100 to $150 (*e.g.* through offering a new higher-end product line or increasing add-on sales) even if prospect traffic remained constant at 1,000 and conversion rate at 50%, then she could achieve $75,000 in sales again.

$$\$75,000 = 1,000 \times 50\% \times \boxed{\$150}$$

4. Any combination of the other variables

As demonstrated, increasing any of the three variables can have a positive impact on sales performance (assuming the other two variables remain constant). However, if a retailer can positively impact more than one variable, the result is a "multiplier effect" that can produce a dramatic impact on sales performance. For example, if the retailer could increase her conversion rate by an additional ten percentage points to 60% and drive 500 incremental prospects into her store (*i.e.* from 1000 to 1500), even holding the average sale constant, the net effect on sales is significant.

$$\$90,000 = \boxed{1,500 \times 60\%} \times \$100$$

Sales Conversion: Final Thoughts

As we have demonstrated, there are a number of ways retailers can drive sales results, but focusing on sales conversion is among the most important—in fact, I think it's the most important. Why? Driving more traffic into your store is great and trying to increase average sale values is important, no question about it. However, sales conversion really speaks to making the most out of the opportunity you have. Whereas driving more traffic usually requires an investment in advertising and trying to drive up average sale values is often a function of your product mix, focusing on sales conversion doesn't necessarily cost you more—you already have the staff, inventory, and merchandising. Sales conversion simply forces retailers to think about how to be more effective with what they have.

As the chart in Figure 4-14 shows, we can readily see how each variable in the sales performance equation contributes to the end sales result. In this case, traffic increased, sales conversion rates increased while average sale value remained flat. This pattern could result from a retailer heavily promoting a sales event featuring "loss leader" products. Though more people visited the store and actually made a purchase, they tended to buy the lower valued items. In the next example in Figure 4-15, traffic was flat, however conversion rates and average sale values increased. In this case, the advertising may have attracted more qualified buyers—though the total traffic volume didn't increase, more of the prospects who visited did make a purchase, and they bought more or higher value items.

By breaking the sales result into these three underlying variables as shown in Figure 4-16, retailers will understand how the sales results are being driven, and consequently be in a far better position to influence the outcome.

Underlying drivers to sales results—increased traffic and sales conversion; flat average sale values

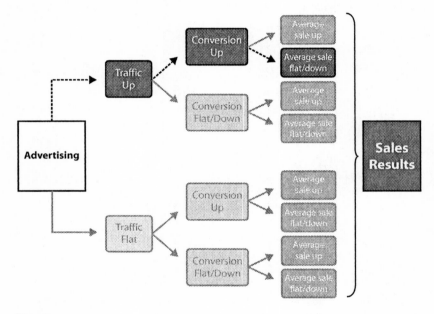

Figure 4-14

**Underlying drivers to sales results—flat traffic;
increased sales conversion and average sale values**

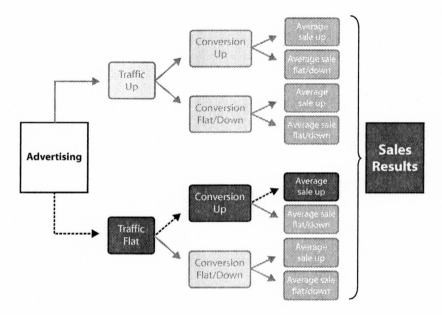

Figure 4-15

Underlying drivers to sales results

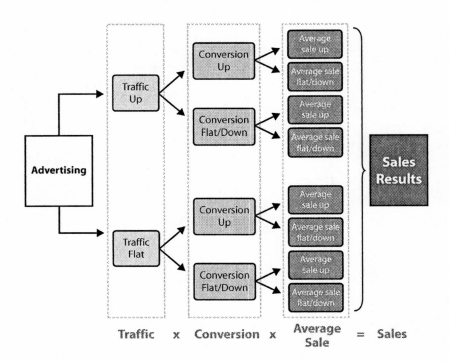

Figure 4-16

Chapter Summary

- Sales conversion is among the most critical retail metrics. Unfortunately, most retailers can't tell you what their sales conversion rate is. They can't tell you because they don't track traffic, and without knowing traffic, they can't calculate sales conversion.

- Sales conversion is simply calculated by dividing total transactions by total traffic and is represented as a percentage of total traffic. For example, if 1,000 prospects visit a retail store and at the end of the day 500 sales transactions are made, then that retailer's conversion rate is 500/1000 = 50%. As the formula implies, without knowing traffic, you cannot calculate conversion.

- Some retailers are so focused on sales growth that they don't believe that conversion rates tell them anything that they don't already know. However, sales alone cannot provide any insight about how the retailer performed compared to the sales opportunity.

- Given that traffic counts are essential in calculating conversion rates, retailers need to start by counting traffic. There are a number of ways they can do this, including electronic traffic counting devices, mechanical turnstiles and manually. Getting a precise traffic count can be tricky. There are a number of factors that can impact traffic counts, including staff movements, non-prospect traffic, prospect movements, buying group size and more. However, there are a number of strategies that can be used to help clarify the traffic data and provide retailers with a useful traffic measure.

- Sales conversion is not about the customers who make a purchase, but rather those prospects that visit your store and don't purchase. There are a number of factors that impact sales conversion, including sales staff effectiveness, staffing levels, merchandising, till availability, promotional strategy, product mix, inventory levels, pricing, buying group size, and the competitive environment.

- In order to drive sales performance, retailers need to understand the variables that drive sales: traffic volume, sales conversion, and average sale value. These variables can be expressed as a formula as follows:

$$\textbf{Sales Revenue } = \textbf{Traffic} \times \textbf{Conversion} \times \frac{\textbf{Average}}{\textbf{Sale Value}}$$

- By positively influencing any of these three variables (while the others remain constant), a retailer can drive sales performance. If a retailer can positively influence two or more of these variables, the result is a multiplier effect whereby the sales result is even more positively impacted.

- Although all three variables are important, sales conversion is particularly critical because it is the one variable that retailers have the most ability to influence—and it doesn't necessarily take additional investments to do it.

CHAPTER

Staff Planning

Staff optimization is not about reducing staff—it's about having the right number of staff at the right time in the right place.

Staff Planning

AT ONE TIME OR ANOTHER, we've all been at that store. Perhaps it was the television ad we saw the night before, or perhaps it was the flyer that fell out of the morning paper. But whatever it was, it worked—because now we're actually there, looking for that limited time special on widgets. And that's when things start to go awry. Perhaps it's because we can't find what we're looking for. Or it might be that we did actually find the widget section, but suddenly realized that we're not quite certain what size we really need. "If I could just find a salesperson," we say to ourselves, twisting our head left and right in the hope of actually seeing someone wearing the store colors. Then, after a moment or two of searching to no avail, we realize the plain truth: "I guess I can come back and get it later." Sure, we can come back later. The problem, from the retailer's point of view, is that we often don't.

STAFF PLANNING

- Staffing and traffic
- Traffic velocity
- Refining staff schedules
- Sales conversion and staffing
- Staffing by gut
- Staff balancing
- Creating staffing guidelines

If there is an unforgivable sin in retail, it is certainly what was just described in the paragraph above. If retail was a spectator sport, this would be the equivalent of watching your favorite baseball team make it to the World Series, only to strike out in the ninth inning and lose by one run. It doesn't really matter that they lost by a single run—the point is, they lost. In this case, they lost the sale. They may have even lost the customer.

The full extent of the tragedy comes from the irony of knowing how much was invested, only to see it all thrown away at the moment of truth. So much cost and effort goes into branding, advertising, and promoting a store and its products, all with the aim of acquiring new, incremental customers. And when they finally respond by coming into the store, they are generally predisposed to either buy or at least seriously consider a purchase. Given what it cost to get them there, it's absurd that any retailer would willingly let them walk away disappointed.

And yet, as every retailer knows, staffing costs money, lots of money. Staffing is, in fact, the single largest operating expense on most retailers' financial statements. Having insufficient staff is disastrous, but then so is having too many staff. So what is a retailer to do?

In this chapter, we will consider the problem of staff scheduling and optimization. As we will see, the answer lies in traffic patterns.

Staffing and traffic

Let's start by looking at traffic by day of week for an average week for a particular retailer. As shown in Figure 5-1, at store A, Mondays start relatively strong, dropping off through the middle of the week, and then ramping up through Friday and peaking on Saturdays. As the manager, if this was all the information you had for staff planning, you would be relatively well-armed to devise an effective staff schedule for the coming week.

Staffing to traffic volume is not a particularly difficult concept; in fact, it is quite intuitive. In this case, the manager will want to ensure that she has enough staff for Saturdays and Sundays—the highest traffic volume days of the week. Furthermore, she'll want to ensure that she doesn't over-staff during the mid-week slump of Tuesday, Wednesday and Thursdays.

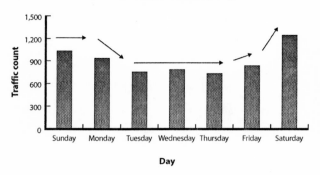

Figure 5-1

One size *doesn't* fit all

Understanding traffic patterns is critical, but don't think that just because you know what the traffic pattern in one store is, it will be the same for all your stores. Every store is different. They're unique. And, consequently, they will have unique traffic patterns. Retail managers need to be aware of this and be careful not to leap to the incorrect conclusion that what happens in one location will be the same for another. Yes, it makes it easier for management to think in

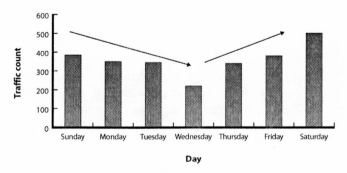

Figure 5-2

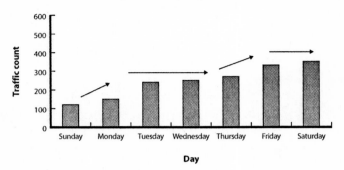

Average traffic by day of week Store B

Figure 5-3

generalizations (especially in large chains), but it will lead to sub-optimal results.

Interestingly, even stores in the same chain and same geographic market have variations in their traffic patterns. The charts in Figures 5-2 and 5-3 show two stores in the same chain located in the same market. As you can clearly see in the weekly traffic distributions, in order to match staff to traffic, each manager will need an entirely different staffing schedule. If this retailer tried to impose a standard schedule, one or the other (and potentially both) stores would be sub-optimizing. Not only are the traffic patterns different by day-of-week, but the total volumes are different as well.

Traffic "velocity": The speed of retail

As demonstrated, having a solid understanding of traffic volume and the timing of prospects in your store is critical to effective staff planning. But in order to fully understand what's going on, you need to dig just a little bit deeper. An example will help make the point.

Let's say you are the store manager and that your average traffic counts by day of week are as shown in the chart in Figure 5-4. Clearly, the busiest day of the week is Saturday—just as it is for many retailers. And, in this case, Sundays have the lowest total traffic counts. This is useful information for planning staff. If you were the manager, how would you plan your staff? Based on total traffic, you obviously need the most staff on Saturdays and the least on Sundays, and something in-between for the other days—right?

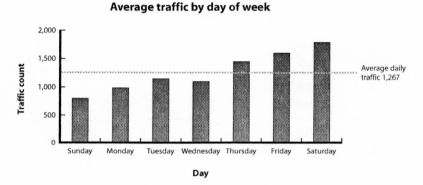

Average traffic by day of week

Figure 5-4

Although this seems quite reasonable based on everything we've said so far, we'll need to dig just a little deeper to be absolutely sure. Here's why.

The days of the week are not necessarily comparable in one very important way: store hours. Most retailers vary the stores hours by the day of the week. The difference in store hours changes the traffic distribution.

In this example, let's say the store hours are as follows:

Another way to look at it would be to say that Monday and Tuesdays have 10 operating hours, Wednesdays through Saturdays have 12 operating hours and Sundays have 5 operating hours—so far, so good. We have summarized the operating hours in Table 5-1.

Table 5-1

Operating hours

Operating Hours
5
10
10
12
12
12
12

Now if we compare traffic volumes to operating hours, not surprisingly, total traffic volumes appear to be related to store operating hours. That is, generally the more hours the store is open, the higher the total traffic. Table 5-2 clearly shows this. This is intuitive, isn't it?

Table 5-2

Operating hours compared to traffic counts

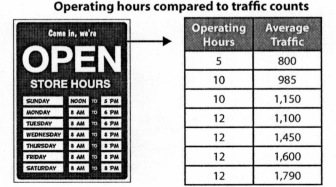

Operating Hours	Average Traffic
5	800
10	985
10	1,150
12	1,100
12	1,450
12	1,600
12	1,790

Now let's divide total daily traffic by the number of operating hours per day and see what our average traffic counts per hour are based on this data. As the Table 5-3 shows, when we look at traffic on a per hour basis, we see that Sunday's average 160 counts per hour. Hey, that's more than Saturday's!

Table 5-3
Traffic velocity by day of week

Average Traffic	Operating Hours	Traffic per Hour
800	5	160
985	10	99
1,150	10	115
1,100	12	92
1,450	12	121
1,600	12	133
1,790	12	149

The highest traffic count per hour or traffic "velocity" occurs on Sundays

Understanding total volume is critical to effective staff planning, but you also need to consider the traffic flow or "velocity," as well. Traffic velocity is simply the average volume of traffic per hour. Notwithstanding the overly scientific sounding term, think of velocity as nothing more than a store's "busy-ness factor." Velocity provides a comparative measure of how busy the store will feel to customers and staff. And part of the beauty is that velocity gives retailers a way to more accurately compare one day of the week to another.

By looking at traffic velocity, a number of important insights become apparent.

The busiest day of the week is actually Sunday. This is the case because, although Sundays do not receive the most total traffic, Sundays actually get the most traffic on a per hour basis. In this example, Sundays received some 160 prospects per hour, whereas Saturdays (which was thought to be the busiest day) receives 149 per hour.

By looking at traffic data in this way, managers can get a more accurate feel for what the day will be like from a traffic perspective. Not only will this type of view reduce or eliminate potentially debilitating under-staffing on Sundays in this example, but also eliminate or reduce the potential overstaffing on Wednesdays. In this case, Wednesdays average only 92 counts per hour during its 12 operating hours, which is about 38% less traffic per hour than Thursdays and Fridays.

Comparing the total traffic by day to the traffic velocity by day as

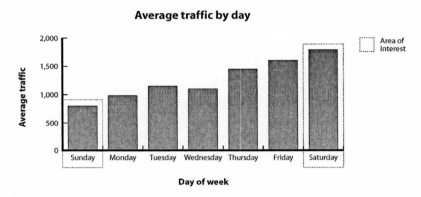

Figure 5-5

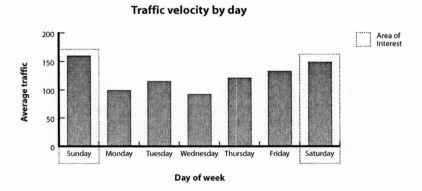

Figure 5-6

shown in Figures 5-5 and 5-6 reveals how different the picture can look when velocity is considered.

Refining the schedule: Hourly traffic distribution

Although general daily traffic patterns are useful for staff planning and traffic velocity is important to understand, the fact is, traffic doesn't happen in nice equal pieces like 130 counts per hour. It's not like 130 prospects gather in the parking lot waiting for the right number and then all decide to come in at the same time. Although traffic velocity provides a quick read on store activity, hourly distribution can be messy.

Hourly traffic distributions can vary considerably; however, they generally fall into one of the three categories shown in Figures 5-7, 5-8 and 5-9:

1. front-end loaded,

2. normally distributed, and

3. back-end loaded.

In order to optimize the staffing schedule, management needs to ensure that there is an adequate staff-to-prospect ratio during each hour of the business day. As the charts below suggest, management will need to schedule staff differently in each case. In a normally

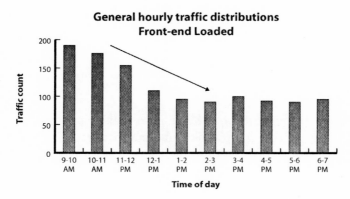

Figure 5-7

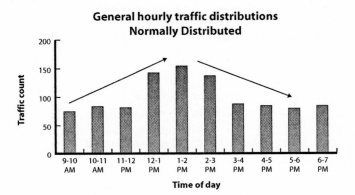

Figure 5-8

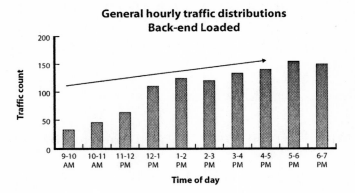

Figure 5-9

distributed traffic pattern, the key is to make sure there is ample coverage through the traffic peak that occurs between noon and 3 PM. In a front-end loaded distribution, the key is to have enough staff at opening and through the early morning hours when traffic is at its highest. And, lastly, in a back-end loaded distribution, the trick is to make sure staffing levels are adequate during the last 3 operating hours.

Consider the following sample traffic distribution shown in Figure 5-10.

In this instance, traffic follows a fairly normal distribution: the morning begins slowly, increases towards mid-day, and then gradually falls off until the store closes. It doesn't take a rocket scientist to realize that staffing requirements in the middle of the day are higher than in either the morning or evening hours. So, if this traffic distribution is predictable and recurring, the wise retailer will plan to have a few additional staff working the floor from 1 PM until 5 PM. And while we're at it, we can also safely assume that we can get by with a skeleton crew during the opening and closing hours.

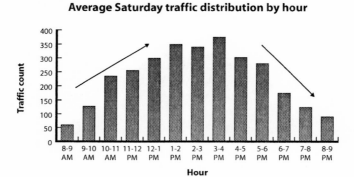

Figure 5-10

Here's another example in Figure 5-11.

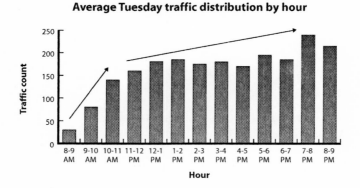

Figure 5-11

This second traffic distribution is more characteristic of a store that has a strong after-work crowd. Here, we see traffic rise throughout the morning, peak at mid-day, but then remain strong right through to the store's closing. In this case, the store can probably get away with a lower staffing level in the morning, but then it's all hands on deck for the rest of the day.

As we've said, it's not that complicated. The only real problem with staffing to traffic volume is simply that many retailers fail to do it because they do not measure traffic in the first place. For those who find themselves in this situation, the most commonly used proxy is sales volume. And that's precisely when things start to go wrong.

To illustrate this point, let's look at an example of hourly sales distribution as shown in Figure 5-12.

As trends go, this is something we've seen before. A slow start that builds to a mid-day peak, which then continues to closing. Fine—

Figure 5-12

that's easy. We just increase staffing in time for the peak, then hold steady for the remaining hours. Right?

Although sales may have peaked in early afternoon, traffic certainly did not—in fact, the traffic was just getting started. "Well, that's certainly interesting," you might say, "but at least the sales are steady." Sure, they're steady. But the real question here isn't how many sales the store is making, but rather how many it's losing.

This is where sales conversion rates once again become a very powerful and insightful tool. In this example, if we divide the hourly sales by the traffic that generated those sales and chart the results, we end up with the graph in Figure 5-13. Suddenly, things aren't looking so good as the day progresses.

In the morning, about 60% of those entering the store make a purchase before leaving. Starting at 12 Noon and through the mid-afternoon hours, however, that percentage begins a rapid descent before bottoming-out at a 45% conversion rate at 3 PM. Conversion rates then increase significantly as traffic levels decline from 5 PM until closing. Clearly, store management would much rather see that 60% conversion figure continue right through the day, but that's not what's happening. Which begs for an answer to the obvious question: "Why not?"

When sales conversion rates shift during the day, there certainly can

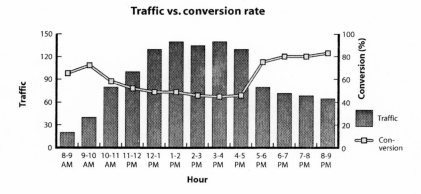

Figure 5-13

be reasons other than staffing. It may be that the size of the buying group (the average number of individuals, usually a family, behind each sale) changes throughout the day. Or maybe there are in-store promotions that only apply to select store hours. Perhaps. In the end, however, more often than not, staffing will provide answers to at least part of the puzzle, and in some cases, all of it.

Conversion—things a little bird told me

In the not-so-distant past, coal miners used to work the mines in the constant company of a canary. Notwithstanding the back-breaking work performed by the miners, it really was the canary that had the worst job. Because whenever the air turned sour, it was the canary that died first. Sales conversion rates are a lot like canaries in that regard—when things start to smell bad, conversion is the first to go.

In the example we've been describing in Figure 5-13, the details are not that unusual. In fact, it's all really quite normal. As traffic increases beyond a certain point, a retailer's ability to convert that traffic into sales begins to diminish. Salespeople can only engage one customer at a time, and there are only so many tills that can be opened. In the end, there are simply a finite number of customers that can be served within a fixed set of store hours and a given staffing level.

Of course, as the number of potential customers in a store increases, there comes a point of diminishing returns. Salespeople become harder to find, and till lineups become longer and longer. Eventually, people will begin to realize that their time is more valuable than the product they came for, and an increasing number of them will leave the store without making a purchase.

The end result of this pattern is the realization that there is an inverse relationship between traffic and sales conversion: as traffic increases, there comes a point where sales conversion will begin to decrease. Conversely, when traffic decreases, conversion will tend to rise. The chart in Figure 5-14 shows a pattern typical of many retail establishments. By ranking daily traffic counts from highest to lowest on one axis, and plotting sales conversion on another, it is easier to see how the relationship works.

Of course, while the chart reveals a general trend, the specifics of the traffic/conversion relationship will vary somewhat for different retailers. It is important to understand that an inverse relationship exists. And since it does, it is imperative for management to do

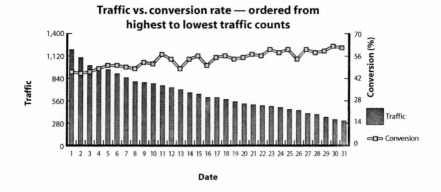

Figure 5-14

everything it can to slow the rate at which sales conversion drops whenever traffic increases. Which brings us back to staffing decisions.

The key to understanding how staffing influences sales conversion (and thereby influences sales) lies in seeing staff availability as a series of constraints. In fact, for those readers with an operational management background, what we're really talking about here is a linear programming problem where the objective is to maximize sales and minimize cost, all the while constrained by finite staffing resources.

For now, though, it is enough simply to understand that staff availability can have a very direct impact upon sales volume. While retail establishments vary in terms of the amount of sales assistance required by the typical customer, every retailer's sales can be bottlenecked by at least some of the following staffing constraints:

- **Floor staff / salespeople**

  While a potential customer may enter a store looking for a particular product, it often requires the assistance of another human being to locate the product, answer questions about it, and even identify related items likely to be of interest. The longer it takes for a salesperson to engage the customer, the more likely it is that the customer will simply leave the store without making a purchase.

- **Cashiers & sales till availability**

  Even in a retail establishment that is able to work entirely on a self-help sales model in which relatively few floor staff are required, staffing can still pose a critical constraint when the would-be customer reaches for his wallet in order to pay for the goods in hand. If the line-up at the till is long enough, there comes a point where the customer realizes that life is too short to spend it in a line waiting to pay money. When you lose the customer at this point it's like—well, there really isn't a sports analogy for this one. It's just wrong, in every meaning of the word.

- **Baggers & carriers**

  While a retailer can generally increase the number of cashiers as needed, there's very little he can do to increase the number of tills once they are all in operation. At that point, if customer line-ups still exist, support staff can be deployed to assist the cashiers by bagging purchases and assisting customers with transporting their purchases out of the store.

- **Customer service**

  When customers return products they have previously purchased at a regular sales till, they obviously impact conversion by taking the cashier's time away from processing new incremental sales. But even when returns are processed at a dedicated returns desk, delays in processing can negatively impact sales volume, particularly in stores where the typical return is accompanied by the customer applying the return credit against the purchase of additional goods or services. Monitoring staffing levels at customer service counters is just as important as cashier tills.

These are just a few tactics that retailers can use to drive performance. Although these may seem pretty obvious to most retailers, without specific measures it is impossible to tell if you're performing well or not. Furthermore, without a means of measurement, you can't tell if any changes you implement are making a difference. Retailers might be very pleasantly surprised at what a difference some of the obvious tactics could have on sales performance.

Staffing by "gut": The way we've always done it

As critically important as optimizing staff scheduling is, many retailers still rely on intuition and heuristics to make their staffing decisions. Like ancient secrets passed down from retail shaman to retail shaman proclaiming that Sunday staffing levels should be no more than five people, because it's been that way forever. There is always room for management experience and "gut" in retail management decision making—but wouldn't it be better to have the data? Furthermore, where gut might be directionally correct, it's never quantitatively specific. Does your gut tell you that you'll have 200 prospects today or will it be 249? There's a big difference.

Since staffing is such a strong influencer of sales conversion rates for many retailers, it stands to reason that studying a store's sales conversion can reveal a great deal about any systematic staffing problems that are creating sales bottlenecks. Consider, for instance, the case of a store having an average weekday conversion chart as shown in Figure 5-15.

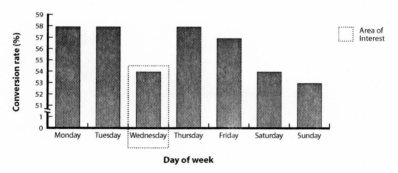

Figure 5-15

With the exception of Wednesdays, Monday through Friday, sales conversion rates are strong and consistent, and then drop on the weekend. This conversion rate pattern may very well provide management with some key insights into staffing effectiveness. For example, what's happening with conversion rates on Wednesdays? Given that staffing is a key factor in driving sales conversion, management should look closely not only at total staffing levels (maybe they're just understaffing) but also look at who they're staffing on these days. It could be that the staff working on Wednesdays are second stringers.

There may be very good reasons for the conversion rates to go down, but by looking at traffic and conversion rates this way, management is in a far better position to pinpoint and resolve the situation—whether it be staffing or some other reason.

Although daily conversion rates can help pinpoint potential staffing issues, for large retailers that have many staff and long store hours, more detailed information may be needed. Figure 5-16 shows conversion rates by hour for a large consumer products retailer. This retailer has up to 24 sales people on the floor at any given time and they operate the store from 9 AM to 9 PM every day of the week. That's a lot of staff and a lot of operating hours. In order to help a retailer in this situation understand potential staffing issues, looking at conversion rates on an hourly basis would be useful. In the example below, conversion rates decrease after 6 PM through to closing. Based on this reoccurring pattern, management hypothesized this lower conversion might have something to do with the fact that the evening shift is usually given to junior employees, as seniority usually dictates scheduling and the more senior staffers don't like working the evening shifts.

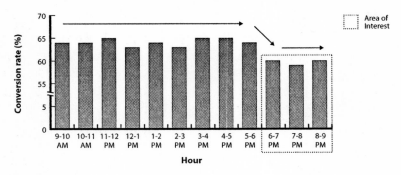

Figure 5-16

Sensing that sales were being negatively impacted by the lack of experience, management decided to plant a few senior staff on the evening shift to see if they could move the sales conversion needle. As the chart in Figure 5-17 shows, sales conversion rates in the evening hours did improve by bringing on the experienced staffers.

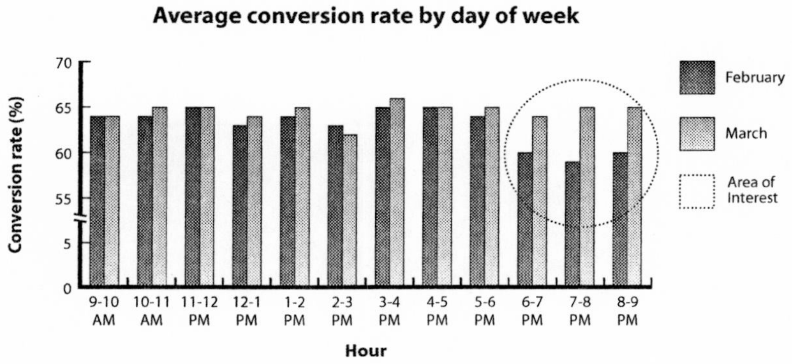

Figure 5-17

The tail wagging the dog

Why it is that maximum prospect traffic in most retail stores coincides with staff lunch breaks? Is it written in stone somewhere that lunch breaks need to happen at noon or 1 PM? As retailers, you control schedules. Yes, people who start work at 8 AM get hungry and need breaks around noon—OK, fine. But if that's when your maximum traffic volume is, don't you think you should do something about it?

Here's an example of what the business impact is of not thinking of customers first. By looking at the chart in Figure 5-18 it is immediately clear that something is happening between 1 PM and 3 PM that is causing sales conversion to drop by nearly 20%.

It is not hard to conclude that staff lunch breaks during the early afternoon period are having an impact on sales conversion rates. Staff need to eat; management needs to run a business. It's not difficult to come up with a compromise that works for staff and ensures that the store is performing the best it can.

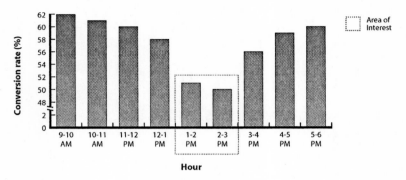

Average conversion rate by hour — Saturdays

Figure 5-18

Staff balancing—we're all in this together

As mentioned previously, each store location is different. Each store will have different daily, and even hourly, traffic distributions. It stands to reason, then, that in order to optimize staffing across a network of stores, there will be differences in staff schedules—where one location has a front-end loaded distribution, another has a normal distribution and a third may have a back-end loaded distribution.

Although staff "balancing" across multiple locations may be impractical for some retailers, it can be extremely valuable for those who can do it. Imagine organizing your entire staff across multiple locations so that you can maximize your sales opportunity simply by redistributing your existing staffing complement to the locations and times where they are needed most. Although you might incur some additional, modest expense in travel costs, you may far exceed this investment with higher sales conversion and higher customer service levels. Here's an example to show you how this could work.

Boxing Day bonanza

In Canada, the day after Christmas, December 26, is called "Boxing Day" and it is among the busiest retail days of the year for many retailers. In order to optimize the sales opportunity that Boxing Day can present, retailers need to be on their toes. Extraordinary events like Boxing Day can really drive management crazy—is it going to be completely mad or just somewhat mad? Last year's sales data alone will not provide management with the perspective they need to make staffing decisions this year. Recollections of traffic by staff won't be precise enough either. Traffic data is the answer.

The following chart in Figure 5-19 shows what happened during Boxing Day in three different locations of a small chain. Although all the stores are located in the same city, the traffic impact was very different by location. Where store #1 was up significantly compared to the average Friday in December, traffic was actually down in store #2 and up only modestly in store #3. Without having traffic data, management might simply staff-up at all locations (it's Boxing Day, of course we're going to be extremely busy!). However, based on last year's traffic volume by store, it's clear that staffing up isn't necessary in all three stores. In fact, management has probably been over staffing in stores #2 and #3.

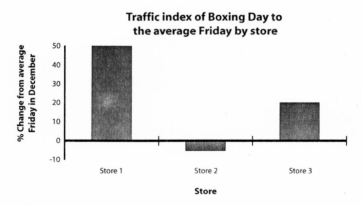

Figure 5-19

Armed with hourly traffic data, management decided to take a closer look at exactly when the traffic occurred for each store last Boxing Day.

As the charts in Figure 5-20, 5-21 and 5-22 show, in addition to the total traffic volume, traffic timing during the day varied considerably by store.

At store #1, traffic was significantly higher than normal during virtually every day-part. Clearly this store had more traffic than it could practically deal with, based on the staffing levels it had.

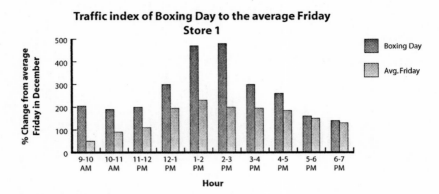

Figure 5-20

In store #2, Boxing Day was a non-event. As the chart clearly shows, Boxing Day traffic was not significantly different than a normal Friday during December, and the store was definitely over-staffed.

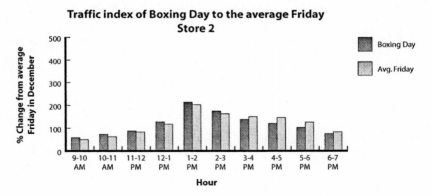

Figure 5-21

In store #3, there was a traffic spike during the opening 3 hours but then traffic levels returned to manageable levels. In this case, store #3 needed the extra staff from 9 AM to 12 PM, but after that, they were probably over-staffed based on the traffic volume.

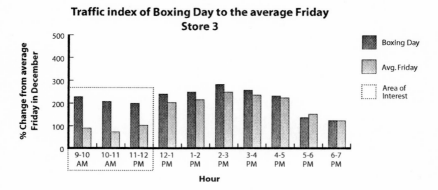

Figure 5-22

By looking at traffic volume and timing, it became clear to management that staff scheduling was not optimal. Naturally, all retailers are concerned about staff expense, but the key, of course, is to make sure you have the right number of staff at the right time, and in this case, at the right location.

For this coming Boxing Day, management has come up with a different staff plan. Specifically, they will actually cut back on the staff at store #2 (assuming that traffic at this location will be low again). The extra staff who would have worked at store #2 will be sent to store #1—the store that really needs the help. Furthermore, a couple of extra heads from store #3 will also be sent to store #1 after the 9 AM to 12 PM rush.

By scheduling staff in this way, management is maximizing the sales opportunity by matching staff to traffic across locations. And, they're not spending any more on staff expense than they did last year!

The good, the bad, and the ugly

Every retailer wants to hire the best people they can; most retailers are challenged with finding great people. This isn't just a retail phenomenon, but retail in particular seems to be a challenge from a recruitment standpoint.

Although traffic analysis can't help with your recruiting efforts, it can help you identify performance opportunities among your staff, so that you can focus your attention on solving the right issues and driving performance. Here's how.

Just as sales conversion can tell you about overall store performance, it can also be used to understand team or even individual employee performance. Here's an example.

Clarion Sound: A case study in measuring sales performance with conversion rates

Clarion Sound offers low to mid-range stereos, home theater systems and televisions. It's a very competitive marketplace, but Clarion Sound has been successful by hiring and retaining knowledgeable and friendly sales staff. In order to compete with the big chains, Clarion Sound maintains extended stores hours—9 AM to 9 PM Monday through Saturday, with limited hours on Sundays. It's a lot of hours for Clarion's nine sales staff.

Using traffic data, management has devised a shift scheduling system that nicely matches sales staff to traffic volumes. The sales team is divided into three teams as detailed in Table 5-4 below:

Table 5-4

Sales teams

Team 1	Team 2	Team 3
Sam	Tom	Rich
Sarah	Brian	Kirsten
Bret	Laurie	Don

During a typical 12 hour operating day, two teams will be assigned to staff the store. One team will work the early morning hours (when traffic volume is modest) and a second team will be brought in at noon to help manage the busy noon to 5 PM period. From 6 PM on, the team that started at noon takes over, and the team that started in the morning goes home for the day. It's a pretty good system.

Management has been looking at sales performance and wondering if it could be better. The company is small, and they're sure that all the salespeople are hard working, good performers, but they need a way to measure. Although the sales data showed that there were only slight differences between the three teams in total sales revenue and margin, management suspected that there may be other differences.

In an effort to better understand team performance, the Controller, was asked to dig into the data. At first glance, she reached the same

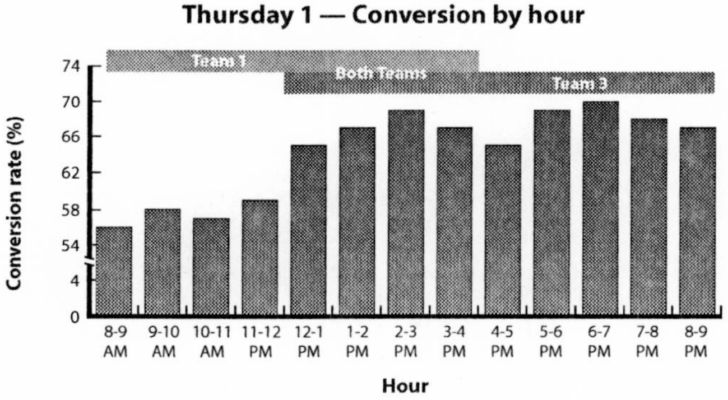

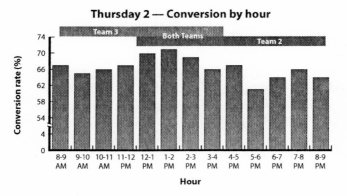

Figure 5-23

Figure 5-24

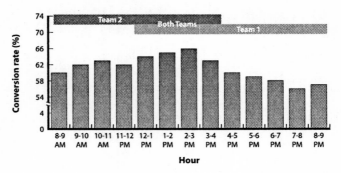

Thursday 3 — Conversion by hour

Figure 5-25

conclusion—all three teams were pretty close in sales and margin performance. According to her analysis, Team 2 was just slightly ahead of Team 3, and Team 1 was only slightly behind team 3. No big issues or opportunities here. Then it occurred to her that it might make sense to look at performance based on sales conversion rates. Perhaps this might provide a different view.

Using the last three Thursdays as a starting point, she plotted teams against conversion rates by hour of day as shown in Figures 5-23, 5-24 and 5-25.

Sales conversion rates by team are summarized in Table 5-5.

Although the teams had comparable performance from a sales revenue and margin perspective, from a sales conversion standpoint, the performance differences were much more significant. Team 3 had an average conversion rate of 68% while Team 2 was 65% and Team 1 was only 62%—6 percentage points less than team 3. Then the Controller broke down the numbers even further in order to isolate performance by team. She removed the combined conversion rates when two teams worked the mid-day shifts, looking only at shifts where one team worked. Looking at conversion rates in this way showed that the performance differences between the teams were even bigger than she had thought, with Team 3 averaging 67% on its own, compared to 63% for Team 2 and only 58% for Team 1. Now management has something to work with.

Table 5-5

Conversion rate by team

Time	Thursday 1 Conversion and Team		Thursday 2 Conversion and Team		Thursday 3 Conversion and Team	
8 - 9 AM	56%	Team 1	67%	Team 3	60%	Team 2
9 - 10 AM	58%	Team 1	65%	Team 3	62%	Team 2
10 - 11 AM	57%	Team 1	66%	Team 3	63%	Team 2
11 - 12 PM	59%	Team 1	67%	Team 3	62%	Team 2
12 - 1 PM	65%	Team 1+3	70%	Team 2+3	64%	Team 1+2
1 - 2 PM	67%	Team 1+3	71%	Team 2+3	65%	Team 1+2
2 - 3 PM	69%	Team 1+3	69%	Team 2+3	66%	Team 1+2
3 - 4 PM	67%	Team 1+3	66%	Team 2+3	63%	Team 1+2
4 - 5 PM	65%	Team 1+3	67%	Team 2+3	60%	Team 1+2
5 - 6 PM	69%	Team 3	61%	Team 2	59%	Team 1
6 - 7 PM	70%	Team 3	64%	Team 2	58%	Team 1
7 - 8 PM	68%	Team 3	66%	Team 2	56%	Team 1
8 - 9 PM	67%	Team 3	64%	Team 2	57%	Team 1

Creating staffing guidelines with traffic data

Understandably, management can't expect individual store managers to make all the right staffing decisions even with the additional insights traffic data can provide. This is especially the case in large chains, where chain-wide policies and procedures are the only practical way to manage the business.

This may sound somewhat contradictory (hey, didn't you just say that every location is completely different and that you can't generalize!?), and it is, sort of. Let me explain.

Every store has a different traffic profile and consequently requires a unique staffing plan. However, management could establish network-wide guidelines that not only provide store level management with direction, but also provide store level managers with some flexibility to optimize for their location. Here's how.

Using traffic information, sales conversion and other performance metrics, management could establish some basic staffing principals that provide a basis for staffing guidelines. For example, the traffic by hour chart in Figure 5-26 below shows what the optimal staff to traffic levels are based on analysis of a number of locations in the chain.

As the chart shows, at traffic levels of 100 or less, two staff members are all that are needed; for traffic levels between 100 to 250, three staff members are needed; at over 250, another salesperson is needed.

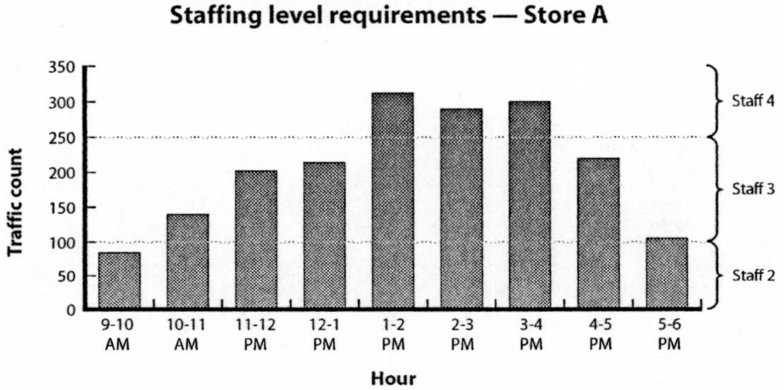

Staffing level requirements — Store A

Figure 5-26

Although it's not foolproof, this approach provides store level management with some basic guidelines to ensure they don't over or under staff. Head office can even factor in mall versus non-mall locations or other physical characteristics that might impact staffing levels to refine the guidelines.

With the following guidelines in place, a store manager at any store in the chain can make rational staffing decisions that help her to optimize staff to traffic for her location, while remaining consistent with head office expectations about staffing levels. Store managers can apply the general guidelines in a customized way—it's the best of both worlds.

Figure 5-27 is a chart for another store in the same chain. Although the traffic pattern is different from the first store, store management can apply the staffing guidelines to their unique traffic and know

Table 5-6

Staffing guidelines

Traffic	Staffing
< 100	2
100 - 250	3
250 +	4

that they're in-line with head office expectations regarding staffing levels.

Staffing level requirements

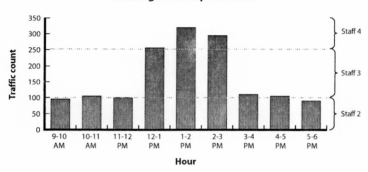

Figure 5-27

Staying flexible—things change, constantly!

Just as traffic patterns vary by store, they also vary month to month, season to season and year to year. Retailers need to stay vigilant in monitoring traffic patterns and adjust as they go. It's not good enough to map traffic patterns for a month or two—if you think that your traffic can be generalized based on such a limited sample, you would be seriously mistaken.

One of the critical variables that changes is the staff itself. Unfortunately, turnover rates in retail tend to be significantly higher than in other industries. As staff changes, sales conversion rates may change, and management needs to watch the trends in order to spot potential staffing issues.

Chapter Summary

- If there is one thing retailers need to get right, it's staffing. Not only does staffing represent the single largest expense for most retailers, staffing also represents the most critical factor in sales performance—even in retail operations with mostly self-help sales.

- General traffic patterns can provide retailers with critical information about the volume and timing of prospects in their stores. The trick is to map staffing to traffic patterns. Unfortunately, it's trickier than it sounds for a couple of reasons. First, every retail location is different. Even stores of the same chain in the same market will have different traffic patterns. The second difference is traffic velocity. Velocity is simply a comparative measure of store "busy-ness" that can be calculated by dividing traffic volume by operating hours. It's important to understand velocity, because days that have relatively low traffic volumes can actually be among the busiest days when velocity is considered.

- In order to optimize staff scheduling, retailers need to look at traffic volumes and patterns on an hourly basis. General daily traffic distributions typically follow one of 3 patterns: normally distributed, front-end loaded or back-end loaded.

- In addition to traffic volume and distribution, it is critical for retailers to understand what their sales conversion rates are by hour. Given the general inverse relationship between traffic volume and sales conversion, retailers need to be on the look-out for anything that can help drive conversion.

- Staff balancing is the process of matching staff levels to traffic volumes across multiple locations. Although staff balancing may be impractical for some retailers, for the ones who can employ staff balancing, the results can be significant.

- Measuring sale staff effectiveness can be a challenge. Although traditional sales metrics like total revenue, sales per customer and so on are useful, none of these traditional metrics provides management with a perspective on how well sales staff are performing relative to the opportunity. By understanding sales conversion rates by employee (or team), management can get a perspective on performance versus the sales opportunity, like never before. Sometimes, good performers are not as good you might think, and under performers may be better than you thought.

- Traffic data can be very useful in creating staffing guidelines for store level managers. Although larger chains may need to impose restrictions in order to maintain overall control, general guidelines can help maintain control while providing store level managers with enough flexibility to optimize staffing levels for their unique location.

- Lastly, it's important for retail managers to stay flexible. The retail environment—both externally and internally—is constantly changing.

CHAPTER

Special Events and Holidays

OK, you know the "Big Sale" is going to be busy, but how busy? Understanding traffic during special events and holidays can help retailers maximize their sales opportunity.

Special Events and Holidays

LET'S FACE IT—people like events and retailers like to create events, but often times the impact of the event is not completely understood by the retailer. The result: less than expected sales and potentially a turn-off for new prospects.

Special events and holidays impact virtually every retailer—some more than others. Christmas is Christmas—it happens every year at the same time, and it pretty much impacts every retailer in some way. St. Patrick's Day is also St. Patrick's Day; it too happens at the same time every year, but it does not impact all retailers in the same way (if at all).

SPECIAL EVENTS AND HOLIDAYS

- Holidays
- Special events
- Making the most of the opportunity
- Multi-location events

Special events and holidays are part of retailing, and retailers need to understand what impact these special events and holidays have on traffic in their stores so that they can make the most of the opportunity from a sales perspective. Unfortunately, many retailers don't fully understand the impact or the opportunity these special events and holidays offer and are destined to keep getting what they expect—probably a lot less than they should.

In this chapter we will describe how holidays and special events impact traffic. From the B-I-G holidays like Christmas, to the events you create exclusively for your store, traffic volume and timing will change (you hope in a positive way), and management's challenge is to maximize the sales opportunity. We'll discuss how managers can do that with the help of traffic analysis.

Holidays

There are holidays and then there are *holidays*, and it is imperative that retailers understand which are which for their store. The fact is, any holiday—statutory, state, provincial, civic, government, religious, school, *etc.*—will change people's behavior and this behavior can (and often does) lead to changes in traffic patterns in your store. These changes can be subtle or dramatic, but either way, a retail manager needs to understand how this will impact his or her store.

- **The BIG ones**

  According to the National Federation of Retail, the biggest retail holidays are, not surprising, the Winter Holidays (*i.e.* Christmas, Hanukkah and Kwanzaa), followed by Back-to-school. One of the key features of these holidays is that they usually include days off work—for non-retail workers, that is. When people have time on their hands, they often spend some of that time shopping.

- **Non-holiday holidays**

  Non-holidays are dates that have some significance and will impact behaviors, but typically less than the big holidays mentioned above: President's Day, Martin Luther King Day, Canada Day, and a whole raft of religious and civic holidays. The fact is, everyone is impacted by holidays—big ones and little ones in some way. Also, the impact will depend upon what it is you sell. Obviously, Mother's Day and Valentine's Day are going to have a profound effect on flower and gift retailers. So, the point here is to understand which kinds of holidays impact your type of store. Most retailers already have a good understanding of which holidays are important to them, but they are less clear about the precise impact.

The impact of holidays on traffic

Holidays, especially holidays where people have days off work and need to buy things—like Christmas—represent the pinnacle of the retailing year for most retailers. People have time (or they make time) to shop. It doesn't get any better than that for retailers! Of course, most retailers will look back on last year's sales data to get some sense of how they should try to manage the coming year's holiday. Unfortunately, sales data alone doesn't provide managers with enough information about:

1. what the opportunity is and

2. how to manage it.

OK, you know Boxing Day is going to be "crazy-busy"—but how do you staff for crazy-busy? Unfortunately, crazy-busy is not a precise or quantitative term.

With traffic data, we can actually quantify crazy-busy. Of course, the traffic impact of any given holiday will be unique to your location. The type of prospects you attract, your physical location (free standing destination versus mall location), your competitive environment will all influence whether or not Boxing Day is crazy, or more or less a regular day. Let's look at some examples.

• **Consumer electronics retailer**

The following chart shows the traffic volume by day during December for a consumer electronics products retailer. As can be seen in the chart in Figure 6-1, traffic at this store most definitely falls into the crazy-busy category! Not only was December a busy month generally for this retailer, but Boxing Day was off-the-chart busy—receiving almost four times the daily average traffic volumes. In fact, Boxing Day represented almost 10% of the entire month's traffic!

December traffic by day

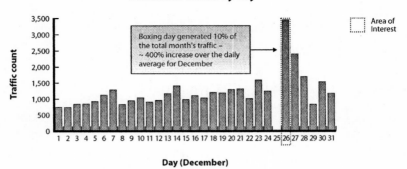

Figure 6-1

• Home improvement retailer

The chart in Figure 6-2 shows what the traffic volume by day during December and Boxing Day might look like for a home improvement retailer. As the chart shows, Boxing Day is not a significant event for this retailer. In this case, Boxing Day traffic was actually down about 19% from the

December traffic by day

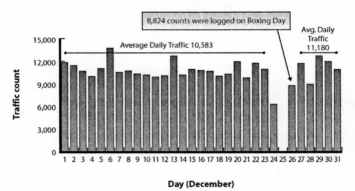

Figure 6-2

daily average during the month! Do you think this might be useful information to the manager as she prepares the staff schedule for next year's Boxing Week?

Being aware that your retail traffic will change (increase or decrease) as a result of a holiday is a small first step. Every retail manager worth his salt should know what the general impact of a holiday is on his business; historical sales data can tell you part of what you need to know. Unfortunately, most managers rely on memory for the rest—"I think we were pretty busy last year ... we'd better staff up." Understanding, and more specifically quantifying, the traffic impact of holidays is critical to managing. But in order to make the information actionable, you need more precise information. Specifically, you need to know what the traffic impact is by hour. Knowing that traffic will be up is part of it, but you also need to know specifically when it will be.

The chart in Figure 6-3 shows traffic volume by hour during Boxing Day. In this case, traffic is up significantly during the first four hours. After these initial four hours, traffic volumes return to more normal levels. This is a critical insight because it enables the manager to refine staffing to ensure she has enough staff to manage the early rush. Obviously, as the day progresses, the staffing levels can be scaled back. Without this information, there is a very good chance the manager will over-staff the entire day.

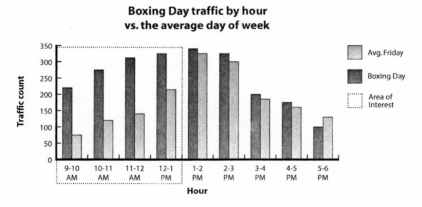

Figure 6-3

Special events

Just like holidays, special events are essentially activities that have an impact on normal traffic volumes and traffic timing. The key is to understand specifically how these special events impact traffic, quantify the impact, and use the information to manage to the best sales result.

So, special events are like holidays in that they represent a change in traffic patterns, but they are different from holidays in one very important way: by definition "special" events are retailer specific. This has a number of important consequences that retailers need to be aware of, including:

- **Retailer driven communications**

  Whereas everyone knows when Boxing Day is (or more typically today, Boxing Week), they may not know when it is Bob's Sport Fishing Customer Appreciation Day. If a retailer creates a special event for his store, the onus is on him to ensure people know about it. For special events, more than ever, the communication and advertising plan, and its execution, are critically important. If you blow the big Boxing Day advertising campaign, there's a good chance traffic will still increase; but if you blow the advertising plan and execution for a customer appreciation event, people just might not show up at all!

- **Competitor response**

  Boxing Day is Boxing Day, and all your competitors know when it happens and are busy trying to figure out how to make the best of it for themselves. Likely, competitors will be less interested in what you're doing for major holidays. Special events are another story. In most cases, when retailers run special events, they need to communicate the details sometime in advance—so prospects can plan to show up. Of course, it's not just prospects that are exposed to your communications. There's not much you can do if your competitor decides to hold a "blow-out" sale event the same weekend as your major customer appreciation event, but you need to keep it in mind. Naturally, this works both ways;

you could always create an event to counter a major event a competitor is promoting as well.

- **Reduced predictability**

  As mentioned above, the major big holidays, and some of the smaller ones for that matter, have certain predictability to them. You may not know precisely how Boxing Day will be this year compared to last year, but if Boxing Day is usually a big traffic day, this pattern should hold in the future. Special events, especially one-off special events, just don't have the same predictability, making these types of events higher risk.

Types of special events

Events and retailing go back probably as far as retailing itself. Of course, a special event is really whatever the retailer says it is. There is no specific criterion for what constitutes a special event, and every day you can find examples of events produced by retailers in your market. In the end, a special event is really only special if prospects believe it's special and show up at your store. If they don't, then I guess it wasn't very special—was it?

Let's look at three of the more common special events retailers hold: grand openings, sales events and new events.

Grand openings

I love grand openings. Where many retail special events are obviously not special and are just ploys to get prospects into their stores (not that this is a bad thing), grand openings are as pure as they get. This is SPECIAL! A new store! Even the grand opening of another location of an existing chain can generate a lot of excitement. To a large extent, retail shoppers have been trained to expect great deals, giveaways, and other treats when they visit a new store. Of course, there's also simple human curiosity at work, as well.

The chart in Figure 6-4 shows the grand opening traffic at a 10-store regional chain. It's not hard to identify the new store on grand opening day compared to the other locations, is it? At over five-times the average traffic levels of the other stores in the chain, it's clear that something really special is going on at this new location.

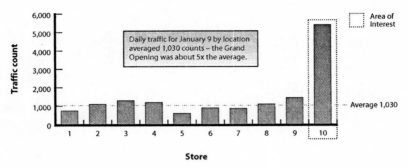

Grand opening store traffic vs. existing locations

Daily traffic for January 9 by location averaged 1,030 counts – the Grand Opening was about 5x the average.

Figure 6-4

A grand opening usually represents among the highest, if not the highest, traffic volume a retailer will ever receive in his location. If a retailer can achieve "grand opening" traffic levels during any subsequent event, that is an impressive feat, and one that is not often accomplished.

Impact of a grand opening on existing locations

Retailers, who have multiple locations in a particular market and open a new location, need to consider the impact that the new store will have on existing locations. Grand openings, in particular, can significantly cannibalize traffic from existing stores, and management will want to understand what the impact is. If the location strategy is sound, the grand opening should have little or no sustained impact on existing store traffic volumes; if it does, that is, if traffic in existing stores merely shifts to the new location, management may have some hard decisions to make going forward.

The charts in Figure 6-5 and 6-6 show the traffic impact on the other two stores in the same chain during the grand opening of the new third location. Although traffic is down over 20% from the prior weeks in both locations, traffic volumes returned to normal levels after the grand opening. In this case, it does not appear that the grand opening has had a permanent impact on traffic levels at the existing stores. Good location decision.

Figure 6-5

Figure 6-6

Sales events

"Truck Load Event," "Spring Sales Event," "Blow-out Sales Event," I think you get the picture. Open your daily newspaper (any day) and you will likely find a retail sales event. Of course, many of these aren't really special sales events; rather, they are everyday pricing all dressed up like a sales event. OK, I can accept that. As retailers we need to create excitement in our stores—sometimes we have to create excitement when there's not a lot to be excited about!

The risk to this, however, is that prospects may show up with expectations of super hot deals, find only your regular stuff with a few scant specials, and refuse to show up next time. "Sales" can make for great events, but only if they meet the expectations of prospects. Like the boy who cried wolf, if you promote sales as events that really aren't, prospects will just stop coming. Fool me once, shame on you; fool me twice, shame on me!

"New" events

Whether it's a new spring collection, a new brand or an entirely new product offering for the store, NEW is a great theme for an event. New events may or may not include a sale component, but when effectively promoted, they can be very effective for event themes. Figure 6-7 shows the impact a new product launch on traffic levels.

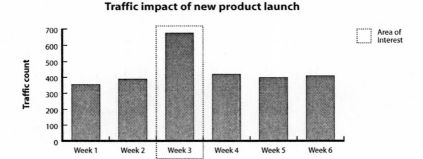

Traffic impact of new product launch

Figure 6-7

Holidays and special event traffic: Final thoughts

As shown, holidays and special events can affect traffic patterns significantly. Although holidays may be more predictable than other special events, armed with historical traffic data, managers can get at least some idea of what might happen to traffic and when. The important thing for managers to keep in mind about traffic response is that traffic patterns are unique by location, so knowing what happened at the downtown store when you run the south side store will not necessarily be helpful. Also, holiday and special event traffic may change year-over-year. Customers change, the competitive environment changes—it all changes, and so do traffic patterns.

"Triage" retailing: Making the most of the opportunity

OK, so you track traffic and expect that the coming Boxing Day is going to look like the chart in Figure 6-8 below. During virtually every day-part, traffic is significantly higher than the normal average for that hour. It would be easy to hopelessly conclude than you and your team are simply going to get creamed, and there's not much you can do about it—or is there?

There is no doubt about it, if you are expecting traffic like the chart below, you are going to get creamed. No retailer can practically staff-up by a factor of three or four as this chart suggests you would need. However, managers are not powerless to influence the outcome of a day like this. There is hope.

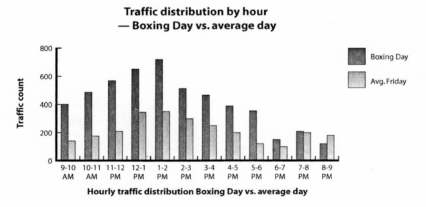

Traffic distribution by hour — Boxing Day vs. average day

Figure 6-8

Addressing the conversion drivers

Let's now examine some of the ways managers can make the most out of these difficult, but potentially tremendous sales opportunities that major events create.

Setting expectations

The old TV sitcom called M*A*S*H, about a medical unit during the Korean War, followed the antics of a group of madcap doctors, nurses and other various characters as they struggled to keep up with the relentless influx of wounded soldiers. One of the ways these characters coped with the hopelessly difficult volume situation was "triage," that is, prioritize. Patients that weren't critically injured were made comfortable, and placed in a holding area. The more critically injured were attended to immediately. Retail managers can use this same triage mentality for dealing with huge traffic increases from holidays or special events.

The first thing to do is set expectations with staff. Let them know that you know that traffic is going to be insane, and that even with best efforts, some customers will not get the kind of service that everyone would like to give. I would even show staff what the traffic chart might look like, so that they can see it for themselves. Engage your staff on the ways that the store could be most effectively managed given the challenging situation—you would be surprised at what great ideas your staff will have.

If all a manager did was to share the traffic data with staff and engage them on how to best deal with it, the store will perform better than it would have otherwise. People tend to rally around causes, and a 400% increase in store traffic is a cause!

Staffing levels

As noted, it is neither practical nor financially reasonable to staff up enough to fully meet the requirements of a holiday or major event traffic. That said, some additional staffing may be absolutely the right answer. Naturally, you will have to understand the expected costs versus financial benefit. Depending upon the type of retail store you operate, you may need to consider customer service staff, sales staff or both.

- **Customer service**

    During major events, you can go along way with adding customer service employees that

    1. help process customer purchases (cashiers/till operators) and

    2. assist prospects with finding what they are looking for.

Ask your cashiers about what they think might speed up processing—consider having one person manage the money and another bagging the purchase, for example. From a customer service perspective, having staff deal with customers in a triage fashion might do the trick. Of course, your staff still needs to deal with customers in a professional and courteous manner, but they can do it efficiently and quickly. During major events, customers also tend to be a little more patient, as long as they can see that the retailer is working hard at trying to serve them.

• **Sales staff**

A huge inflow of prospect traffic can be a windfall for sales staff. The key here might be to provide some additional incentive for them to go above and beyond the call of duty—and to make some extra money at the same time. Holidays or special events might be a great time to try a sales incentive program, if this sort of program is consistent with your company's policies and culture. It's not for everyone. Yes, it will cost you more—after all, these sales people are already going to be making good commissions based on the extra traffic alone, right? The point is, you need a way for the sales people to work even harder. If they can earn a great commission by just showing up, some might be happy with that. But, an added incentive just might put a little extra jump in their step. Yes, it will cost you more, but it may be worth it. For example, if your sales incentive program costs you $5,000 for the day, but you actually generate an incremental $15,000 in net margin, the sales incentive program would be more than worth the cost.

Inventory

I realize this is Retailing 101, but it's worth stating. Having the right inventory or enough inventory for a special event is critical. There is nothing more disturbing to customers than to visit a store for a special event—fighting traffic, crowds, and risking your life for a parking stall, only to find that the store is out of stock of what you wanted. Analyzing last years sales by SKU will be useful, but also look at traffic. If you stocked out of an item last year and made a lot of prospects angry, you wouldn't want to stock to that same level for this year's sale, would you?

In-store marketing and merchandising

The good news is that holidays and special events often bring lots of new prospective customers into your store; the bad news is that, because of the large traffic volumes, your customer service levels are not usually as high as you would like them to be. Because of the high traffic volume, to a greater or lesser extent, prospects are going to have to figure things out for themselves. If your store is hard for prospects to navigate—they can't find products, displays are poorly signed, and things are generally difficult, then people won't or can't buy. Not only will this reduce conversion rates and therefore be a missed sales opportunity, but even more importantly, some of those new prospects just might not want to come back again. And they might tell a few of their friends what a bad experience they had as well. Ouch!

Store hours

Although I don't recommend changing store hours on a whim, it might make sense to change store hours for holidays and special events. Before you actually try this, you might want to look at traffic patterns by hour from the last event to better understand what happened. After reviewing your traffic profile during the last event

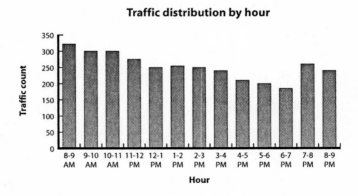

Figure 6-9

(or the previous several events would be even better), you can make a reasonably informed guess about whether or not changing the store hours may make sense for the event. In the chart in Figure 6-9, traffic is obviously ramping down from opening to the evening hours; however, traffic volumes are still very strong from 8 PM to 9 PM—might it have been worth staying open an additional hour?

Ramp-up/Ramp-down

During holidays and special events, there are a million details to manage. Managers are usually running from opening to close. Notwithstanding the intensity of the situation, managers need to watch traffic volumes by hour. If the typical pattern is for traffic to be strong through the first part of the day and then ramp down, managers should plan on adjusting staff schedules accordingly. There's nothing worse than having a successful event, only to eat into the margins by over-staffing during the tail end of the day when staff aren't needed.

Capturing key learnings

The last point is about preparing for the next event. This is easier said than done, given the pace and activity level associated with holidays and special events. But it's important. By documenting key observations, or learnings, during and immediately following the event, management will have tremendously useful information for planning the next event. Relying on recollections like, "Yeah, I think we were really busy," as your only input for planning the next event is not very useful.

Multi-location events

For retailers with multiple locations, the changes in traffic volume and timing created by holidays and special events can be even more challenging. Here's why. Unlike a single location where management has to deal *only* with the traffic situation at hand, in a multiple location retailer, the traffic impacts from holidays and special events can, and often do, vary by store. The charts in Figures 6-10, 6-11 and 6-12 illustrate the point.

On Boxing Day, traffic at store #1 was up significantly across all day-parts. Boxing Day was up 76% compared to the average Friday in December.

Figure 6-10

In store #2, Boxing Day was a very different experience than in store #1. As the chart shows, from 9 AM to 12 PM, traffic was up significantly (about 3 times the average volume), but after the door-crashers were over, traffic volume, though brisk, was not significantly higher than a normal Friday in December.

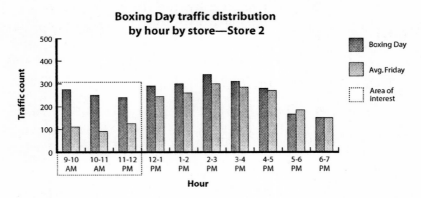

Figure 6-11

In store #3 Boxing Day traffic volumes and distribution were about normal compared to the average traffic for a Friday in December.

In fact, total traffic in this location was actually slightly lower than a typical Friday in December.

Figure 6-12

Managing across multiple stores

At store #1, management's challenge is in trying to make the most out of a significant increase in traffic. In this case, the notion of triage management certainly applies. Boxing Day had a tremendous impact on traffic, and management and store personnel will be scrambling all day to keep up. At store #2, there was an initial spike in traffic and then traffic levels normalized. In this case, store management only needed to employ triage during the first hour or two of the day; after that, it was more or less business as usual. At store #3, it was basically business as usual the entire day. Boxing Day had virtually no impact on traffic levels whatsoever. This variability in traffic response by location is exactly what causes the confusion when it's time to plan for next year's Boxing Day.

Let's say you are the regional manager for these three stores and sit down with the three store managers to discuss this year's Boxing Day experience. Here's what it might sound like.

> **Store Manager #1**: "We got creamed. From the moment we opened until close, the store was packed. We really need to re-think our approach to Boxing Day. We just can't manage the potential business we're getting—I know we could do better if we plan for the increase."

Store Manager #2: "Well I agree with you to a point. The door-crasher specials definitely worked—we got creamed from 9 AM to 12 PM, but after that we were pretty much able to manage the day. If we just focus on those opening couple of hours, I think we'll be alright."

Store Manager #3: "I'm not sure what all the fuss is about. We were ready for anything. Overall the day felt pretty normal. We even managed the morning door-crashers well. I wouldn't say that we got creamed at all. I guess it just comes down to how you manage—we seem to be doing all the right things. I'm not sure I would change a thing."

Without the benefit of traffic information, how could the regional manager actually understand what happened during Boxing Day? How could the individual store managers know what actually happened? By relying only upon the recollections and opinions of the respective store managers, the regional manager might become more confused. Based on traffic analysis, it's clear that all three managers' recollections are correct but different—very different. Assuming that Boxing Day is Boxing Day and that the traffic response in all locations will be more or less similar is dangerous.

As the regional manager, you first need to understand what the traffic response was for each location. As the charts above showed, they were all different. From a traffic perspective, Store #1 clearly did get creamed. In addition to adopting a triage mentality, management might consider staffing up to help support the traffic. In store #2, though the opening hour is very busy, the rest of the day is only marginally higher. Triage management for the first hour or two is all that may be needed. Notwithstanding the store #3 manager's assertions that he was managing well, the fact is, there really wasn't anything special to manage. Traffic was no different than a typical Friday for December—sorry store #3, you're not necessarily a brilliant manager!

Chapter Summary

- Holidays and special events can have a profound impact on traffic volume and timing. In order to make the most of the opportunity that holidays and special events create, management needs to understand the associated traffic impact.

- Holidays change people's behaviors and life patterns, so it makes sense that holidays might impact shopping patterns. The extent to which a holiday will impact traffic in your store will depend on a number of factors, including the type of holiday—ranging from BIG ones like Boxing Day that impact virtually every prospect, to less significant holidays like President's Day or Victoria Day. In addition to the type of holiday, traffic response will vary based on the type of products you sell; some retailers may experience a significant increase (or decrease) in traffic, while it's a typical traffic day for others.

- Special events are different from holidays in that they don't necessarily happen on a specific date each year, and they are retailer-specific. This is a big difference. Because special events are driven by the retailer, there are a number of consequences that need to be kept in mind. First, all the communications for the event will need to come from the retailer, and consequently, if the communication strategy or execution is not done well, the special event will not be successful. Second, special events can be targeted by competitors because they are usually promoted to prospects in advance. And third, unlike holidays that tend to have more consistent traffic patterns year-over-year, special events are far more unpredictable from a traffic response perspective. Special events are as unique as retail itself; three of the more common types of special events are grand openings, sales events and any event that promotes something new.

- Managing holidays or special events can be a significant challenge. When a holiday or special event drives traffic levels up significantly, management should employ a triage approach. As part of this approach, management should start by setting expectations with staff about how the increased traffic should be dealt with. Next, management should review staffing levels, inventory levels, in-store marketing, merchandising, and store hours. Adjustments will likely need to be made to maximize the sales opportunity that holidays or special events can present.

• Managing multiple locations during holidays or special events can be especially challenging. Often the traffic response during a holiday or special event is different by location. Management needs to understand specifically how it is different and employ strategies in each location that will maximize the sales opportunity, whether that requires a staffing increase, heightening awareness, operating in a triage mode or doing nothing.

CHAPTER

Multi-location Traffic Analysis

Whether you have 2 or 200 stores,
the more locations you have,
the more challenging the traffic
analysis will be—and the more
valuable the traffic insights!

Multi-location Traffic Analysis

THE IDEA OF MULTI-LOCATION TRAFFIC ANALYSIS isn't something for only the largest goliaths of retail to be concerned with. In many ways, smaller chains with, say 10 sites, often have the greatest challenge. On the one hand, they are not small operations, and the complexity has really started to set in; on the other hand, retailers of this size are usually still trying to manage the operation as a small business.

MULTI-LOCATION

• Multi-location challenge

• Types of locations

• Performance metrics

• One size doesn't fit all

• Performance management

You know, managers wearing too many hats, managing too many details, and generally letting the business run them. The idea of traffic analysis is right up there with quantitative marketing research, brand strategy, and store atmospherics—it's all pretty cool stuff, but not something these managers have time for. As one manager summed it up, "I don't have time to look at this kind of stuff—I'm too busy running my stores."

Of course, large retail operations need traffic analysis even more than smaller operations. The fact is, if you look at the type of retailer who monitors retail traffic today, you'll often find that it is the larger retail chains. Maybe it's partly why they are now big retailers instead of small retailers?

The good news is that a larger percentage of retailers actually do monitor traffic in their stores; the bad news is that many of them don't do very much with the traffic data they collect. Collecting traffic data is the easy part; turning the data into information and doing something meaningful with it is the hard part.

In this chapter we review the challenges and significant benefits multi-location retailers can realize through traffic analysis.

The multi-location challenge

The fact is, traffic analysis for multiple locations can get a little complicated—even two locations qualify. Essentially, everything that we have covered thus far and everything yet to come, all applies—but now you have the added burden of extending these concepts and analysis over a number of sites and among the sites! As previously noted, every location is unique. Even stores in the same chain in the same market can exhibit different traffic patterns, and consequently require a different management imperative. OK, before you put the book down in hopeless resignation, hold on. It may not be as bad as you think. Yes, multi-location traffic analysis is harder, but you don't need to make a career out of it in order to gain meaningful insights. We'll show you how.

Types of locations

Although this seems pretty obvious, let's start by reviewing the characteristics of multi-location retailers. The fact is, the traffic analysis complexity does vary depending on the chain characteristics, number of sites and geographical distribution. Let's start with some definitions.

- **Local chains**

    A local chain is defined as a group of stores (two or more) where all the stores are located in the same trading area.

Trading Area

For practical purposes, our definition of trading area is a geographic area that is generally subject to the same economic, competitive and weather conditions.

For example, Kansas City would be considered the trading area for a chain of stores all located in Kansas City and the immediate area. However, a chain located throughout the Greater Toronto Area (GTA), which is comprised of several cities, might be thought of as a regional chain. Thinking of a trading area as a city is about right.

- **Regional chains**

  In this case, the chain has locations in multiple trading areas, but is not national in scope. This could be a chain with multiple locations in the same state or province, for example, Templeton Hardware and Lumber with 18 stores throughout the state of Texas. Or, a regional chain could also have stores in multiple provinces or states, for example, The Fishing Spot, with 20 locations in Western Canada.

- **National chains**

  Although there is no strict definition of national *per se*, major retailers usually refer to themselves as national if they have locations in all or most major markets in a country.

- **Store formats**

  By store format, we are referring to the physical characteristics of the retail stores themselves. Some chains strive for a consistent look and feel for each location. Although there may be slight differences among the stores, essentially, they are more or less the same. Other chains have different classifications of store formats that often relate to store size, inventory levels, product mix and sometimes services. For example, the Mega Box Computer retail chain designates stores in their chain as A, B, C and D. A stores are the largest stores, with 30,000 square feet or more of selling space.

They carry the entire range of Mega Box Computer products and maintain large quantities of inventory on-hand. Furthermore, A stores offer in-store technical service and warranty repairs. The Mega Box Computer D stores are usually located in strip malls with less than 5,000 square feet of selling space. These stores only carry the top-selling product lines and they do not offer technical or warranty service.

• **Store banners or brands**

Some chains actually have multiple store brands or banners as part of their chain. You can think of these as chains within chains. For example, a chain called National Books has three different banners as part of their chain: National Books (book superstores located in major markets across the United States), Readers (mid-sized book stores located in some major and many secondary markets), and The Book Stop (shopping mall based book stores located through the Eastern seaboard). Table 7-1 summarizes general chain store characteristics.

Table 7-1
General retail chain characteristics

Chain Characteristics

	Standard Format	Single Banner	Multiple Formats	Multiple Banners
National Chain				
Regional Chain				
Local Chain				

Number of sites and Geography

Context for multi-location traffic analysis

As Table 7-2 shows, the combinations and permutations are many. Although local chains that have a standard format and a single banner are easier to manage from a traffic analysis perspective, it doesn't mean it's necessarily simple. A local chain could have 20 stores—there's nothing simple about 20 stores!

The critical consideration in multi-location traffic analysis is, as much as possible, to conduct the analysis comparing stores with similar characteristics. For example, traffic patterns in a Mega Box Computer A format store will be different than a Mega Box Computer D format store. Obviously total traffic volume will be different (well it better be higher in the A store or Mega Box Computers has a big problem), but there will likely be other differences including traffic timing and sales conversion rates.

Table 7-2
Retail chain traffic analysis complexity

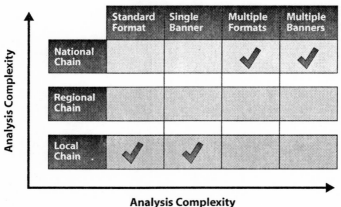

Analysis Complexity

Head office versus store level view

Of course there are many stakeholders of traffic information in a retail organization. Figure 7-1 shows some of the traffic data stakeholders. Let's start by breaking it out into the two fundamental stakeholder groups:

1. head office and

2. store level.

Head office

The term head office in this context really refers to any stakeholder besides the individual store-level personnel. These key stakeholders are shown in Figure 7-1.

Retail chain traffic information stakeholders

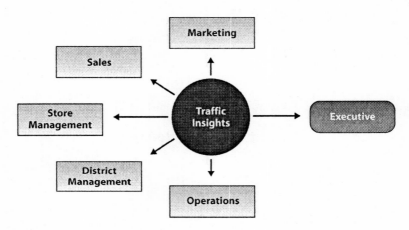

Figure 7-1

Regional management

Depending upon the size of the chain, stores are often divided up into regions or territories, and regional managers usually have responsibility for the stores in their region. This responsibility can range from a few locations to 100 locations. Typically, regional managers are interested in the overall performance of the group. To drive overall group performance, the regional manager needs to have a solid understanding of individual store performance so that she can identify top and bottom performing stores. Traffic analysis can be very helpful to the regional manager for this purpose.

Operations management

Again, specific responsibilities for operations will vary from chain to chain; however, the operations group is often concerned with efficiencies across the network. The operations team might use traffic information for such areas as analyzing general staffing levels, refining store hours, and evaluating location strategies.

Marketing and Sales:

• Marketing

As discussed in *Chapter 1*, advertising is a significant expense for retailers. This tends to be the case especially for chains, as large retail businesses are usually big advertisers. In this case, head office marketing management would be keenly interested in how their advertising programs pull traffic into the locations. Furthermore, marketing would want to understand the relative performance of various media or promotions, and the impact of advertising on different geographic regions, formats, and banners. Marketing can also use traffic data for understanding the impact of competitors and conducting market analysis and forecasting.

• Sales

Head office sales management will be concerned with sales conversion rates across the chain. With this, sales management can formulate strategies to help the stores drive sales performance, including sales training, incentive programs, and compensation plans.

Executive management

Senior executives are naturally interested in the overall performance of the chain, but will likely want a higher-level, more strategic view of the traffic analysis. This will be covered in detail in *Chapter 9: The Strategic Value of Traffic Insights*; however, some of the areas executive management may be interested in are location strategies, long-term traffic and business trends.

Store level stakeholders

Depending upon the size of the individual stores in the chain, the store level stakeholders could be one or several people. For example, a large sporting goods retailer may have several department managers within the store. Naturally, store level management is concerned with the "in the trench" tactics and execution of running the store.

From a traffic analysis perspective, the two key areas of store level management focus are:

1. sales performance and

2. staff scheduling and planning.

Traffic analysis view summary

As Figure 7-2 shows us, there are many potential stakeholders for traffic analysis within a retail chain organization. Of course, it's critically important for the store level management to be armed with traffic analysis so that they can run their stores as efficiently and effectively as possible. As illustrated, there are many important uses for traffic analysis at head office. Traffic analysis can play a significant role in everything from performance benchmarking and

Organization wide traffic information applications

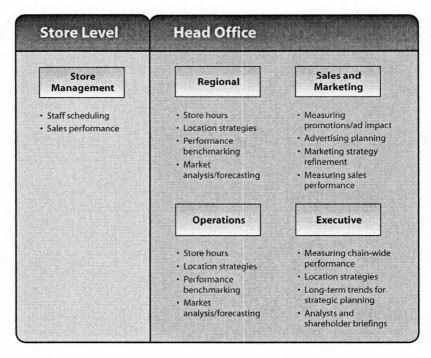

Figure 7-2

market analysis to strategic planning at the highest levels of the executive management.

While some retail chains rely heavily on traffic analysis, others, apparently either don't do it at all or use traffic data in only a very limited way. Of the many potential uses for traffic data, none is more critical than measuring performance—which is where we will turn our attention next.

Multi-location performance metrics

All kinds of interesting and useful metrics and statistics have been devised to help retailers with multiple locations measure performance. Revenue per square foot, revenue per employee, average sale, average margin, number of transactions, average number of lines per receipt, to name a few. Of course, overall sales revenue tends to be the most used, and this makes a lot of sense. If one location has higher sales than another location, the store with the higher sales is thought to be the better performing location. It makes sense, doesn't it? As illustrated in *Chapter 4: Sales Conversion*, sales revenue alone falls short of giving the retailer a clear sense of what the true performance is. It's scary to think of a 40 store chain where management really doesn't know how the locations are actually performing.

If a chain store organization is using sales revenue as its primary measurement for determining comparative store performance (and many indeed do), they're just not getting a complete picture about performance. And, in fact, they could be drawing completely wrong conclusions about which are the top and bottom performing locations. This distortion of performance can lead management, as they attempt to implement strategies to drive sales performance, to implement the wrong fixes. It would be like a doctor prescribing a medication for a misdiagnosed medical condition. The exact outcome may be a little hard to predict, but quite likely the patient is not going to get better! Using sales conversion, along with other measures, can certainly go a long way in helping retail management diagnose each location properly and provide the basis by which an effective treatment can be prescribed.

We'll now explore the idea of multi-location performance in the context of a case study.

Richard's Sport Shops: A case study in multi-location performance

Richard's Sport Shops have been around for a long time—21 years to be precise. Growing from a single small store in Seattle, Richard Isaac built his sporting goods business into a 12 location regional chain operating throughout the Northwest. Although the business has grown nicely, notwithstanding the very tight margins, Richard continues to challenge his management team to drive sales performance. Although Richard is proud of the retail "dashboard" he and his team have devised to help them better understand store level performance, he's concerned that they have plateaued. Nothing seems to be working. All the old strategies just don't seem to be having the same impact and Richard is starting to get worried that the business is hitting a wall. Richard is quickly coming to the conclusion that the only way they're going to be able to drive sales revenue growth is by opening additional stores.

Figure 7-3

Of the several Key Performance Indicators (KPIs) Richard's management team uses, none are more important than overall Sales Revenue and Average Sale per Customer.

As Table 7-3 shows, the sales for last month are detailed by store. Although there is some variation month-to-month, generally, the overall rankings don't seem to change much. Seattle store #2 always seems to have the highest revenue and Portland store #1 usually comes in second.

Table 7-3

Monthly sales by store

Store	Sales
Seattle #2	**$378,000**
Portland #1	**$289,000**
Seattle #1	$240,000
Boise #2	$198,000
Tacoma #1	$183,000
Portland #2	$177,000
Seattle #3	$158,900
Great Falls	$155,000
Boise #1	$151,500
Spokane	$138,900
Tacoma #2	$137,200
Cheyenne	$129,500

When management compares stores based on Average Sale per Customer, as shown in Table 7-4, the rank does change. As the table below shows, Seattle store #2 and Portland store #1 are in the middle of the pack. But, because they deliver so much total revenue, coming up a little short on the Average Sale per Customer metric isn't the end of the world. In fact, store management in both of these locations is really working on trying to get their Average Sale per Customer numbers up—progress is being made, albeit slowly.

Based on the urging from Richard's Boise store #1 manager, Merrell, traffic counters were installed across the chain so that traffic volumes could be included in the performance dashboard, as well. Merrell had a crack team at his store. He knew he ran a tight ship—customers were being well served (customer satisfaction surveys supported this) and his Average Sale per Customer was

Table 7-4

Average sale by store

Store	Average Sale
Tacoma #1	$72.00
Tacoma #2	$69.00
Boise #1	$68.00
Cheyenne	$67.00
Portland #1	**$63.00**
Boise #2	$62.00
Great Falls	$62.00
Seattle #2	**$61.00**
Seattle #3	$60.00
Seattle #1	$58.00
Spokane	$57.00
Portland #2	$56.00

among the highest in the chain. Unfortunately for him, though, total revenue was consistently among the bottom third.

Richard was well aware of the performance at Boise store #1. They had tried all kinds of sales training and other tactics to drive overall sales, but he had resigned himself to the fact that Boise store #1 was never going to be a top performing location. It was, after all, slightly smaller than Seattle store #2 and Portland store #1—how could it possibly generate the same sales revenue as these larger stores? Richard was skeptical, but agreed to go along with the traffic counting anyway—it did make some sense to count traffic, at least to help with staff scheduling.

For the first time ever, management now had traffic counts by location to consider as part of their operational reviews. The traffic counts per location are listed in Table 7-5.

Table 7-5

Monthly traffic counts by store

Store	Traffic
Seattle #2	**22,130**
Portland #1	**18,350**
Seattle #1	15,325
Boise #2	9,120
Portland #2	8,320
Seattle #3	8,300
Spokane	8,125
Great Falls	6,250
Tacoma #1	6,200
Tacoma #2	5,230
Cheyenne	5,225
Boise #1	**5,180**

The additional information was intriguing. Not surprisingly, Seattle store #2 and Portland store #1 indeed had the highest traffic levels. But it was surprising that Boise #1 had the lowest traffic in the chain. It was even more surprising given that sales for Boise store #1 are not last. Merrell felt gratified to know that he was apparently doing a good job. His sales revenue was not last, but his store was actually getting the least amount of prospect traffic. The managers for Seattle store #2 and Portland store #1 weren't convinced that this additional traffic information really proved much. Yes, it was a fact that their stores received the most prospect traffic, but they also delivered the most revenue—it's relative. It all made perfect sense, didn't it?

Armed with traffic data, management was able to calculate one last important statistic—sales conversion. Average sales conversion rates by store are detailed in Table 7-6.

Table 7-6

Average sales conversion rate by store

Store	Conversion
Boise #1	43%
Tacoma #1	41%
Great Falls	40%
Tacoma #2	38%
Portland #2	38%
Cheyenne	37%
Boise #2	35%
Seattle #3	32%
Spokane	30%
Seattle #2	28%
Seattle #1	27%
Portland #1	25%

Although the traffic counts were interesting, sales conversion literally changed the world order at Richard's Sport Shops. As the conversion rate data clearly shows, Seattle store #2 and Portland store #1 were actually in the bottom third of the stores and Boise store #1 was had the highest conversion rate in the chain—in terms of sales conversion, Boise store #1 was the best performing store!

Putting all the pieces together like in Table 7-7, along with other KPIs the chain had already been tracking, Richard was surprised not only in terms of which his top performing stores were, but more importantly, in terms of what the true sales revenue opportunity actually might be. By monitoring traffic, conversion, and average sale along with the resultant sales revenue, management now had a more complete picture of store level performance.

Based on the new conversion rate data, the average sales conversion

Table 7-7

All performance metrics by store

Store	Sales	Store	Traffic	Store	Conver-sion	Store	Average Sale
Seattle #2	$378,000	Seattle #2	22,130	Boise #1	43%	Tacoma #1	$72.00
Portland #1	$289,000	Portland #1	18,350	Tacoma #1	41%	Tacoma #2	$69.00
Seattle #1	$240,000	Seattle #1	15,325	Great Falls	40%	Boise #1	$68.00
Boise #2	$198,000	Boise #2	9,120	Tacoma #2	38%	Cheyenne	$67.00
Tacoma #1	$183,000	Portland #2	8,320	Portland #2	38%	Portland #1	$63.00
Portland #2	$177,000	Seattle #3	8,300	Cheyenne	37%	Boise #2	$62.00
Seattle #3	$158,900	Spokane	8,125	Boise #2	35%	Great Falls	$62.00
Great Falls	$155,000	Great Falls	6,250	Seattle #3	32%	Seattle #2	$61.00
Boise #1	$151,500	Tacoma #1	6,200	Spokane	30%	Seattle #3	$60.00
Spokane	$138,900	Tacoma #2	5,230	Seattle #2	28%	Seattle #1	$58.00
Tacoma #2	$137,200	Cheyenne	5,225	Seattle #1	27%	Spokane	$57.00
Cheyenne	$129,500	Boise #1	5,180	Portland #1	25%	Portland #2	$56.00

rate across the chain was 35%. However, his top three stores had conversion rates of 40% or better. If he could find a way to increase conversion rates across the chain by even 5%, from 35% to 40% on average, the incremental sales revenue would be significant. Maybe there was hope after all!

One size *doesn't* fit all management strategies

Unfortunately, multiple site retailers often assume that one strategy or approach can be applied across all locations and the outcome will be similarly positive in every location. Generalizing performance issues and tactics for improvement across a chain can be extremely counter-productive and even detrimental to the business. For example, it would not be uncommon to hear the following discussion at a meeting of senior retail management regarding sales performance across the chain:

CEO: "The numbers are in and it doesn't look great. We're coming up short of our Q3 target and year-over-year performance is off, as well. We need to do something. Ideas?"

VP Marketing: "Our advertising spending is up about 5% from last year at this time—I feel comfortable with our investment level. I am confident that our new flyer design and schedule are working well—I've had great feedback from a number of store managers. They are pleased and tell me that customers are walking into the store, flyer in hand."

VP Operations: "The competition is coming on stronger than ever. Their store renovation program and new high line of products are really starting to hurt. Our stores look good, but a few of them are a little tired."

VP Sales: "I'm a little concerned about our Average Sale per Customer numbers—we must do a better job of up-selling and cross-selling customers. There is no reason why customers who come in and buy a system shouldn't also buy accessories. It should be an easy add-on!"

CEO: "I'm not convinced that the our performance is being affected by a few tired looking stores. Our merchandising is solid. And as far as the competition is concerned, there's nothing we can do about them. I agree that our marketing spend feels about right—and I like the new flyer look too. I'm not surprised that the feedback has been positive. Sales—now there's an area to work on. Not only is Average Sale per Customer down from last year, but the number of items per sale are also down. We need to do something on the sales front. Thoughts?"

VP Sales: "I've just received some information on a new sales training program that focuses exclusively on up-selling and cross-selling—it looks pretty good."

CEO: "Notwithstanding the cost of the program, which we'll need to check-in with Finance on, this feels like the right approach. How long will it take to get implemented across all the stores?"

The scenario above is far more common than you might expect. When you are managing a chain, and particularly a larger chain, to an extent, generalization is the only practical way to manage the complexity. Although it's easy to see how management gets to these "one size fits all" solutions, it's tantamount to a doctor prescribing the exact medication to 50 patients who happen to be in the same ward. Just because they're in the same ward doesn't mean the same treatment will work the same for all patients. In fact, it's not hard to imagine that this "cookie-cutter" approach to medicine would be seen as a form of reckless malpractice. It's curious then why so many retail organizations think they can do the same thing. In this case, the patient may not die, but she quite likely won't be getting any better either.

Driving sales performance

As shown in Figure 7-4, driving sales performance across a retail chain requires:

Performance improvement framework

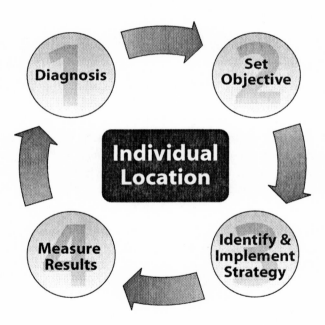

Figure 7-4

1. proper diagnosis of the problem for each location,

2. setting an objective for change,

3. formulating an effective strategy to achieve the objective and implementing the strategy, and

4. measuring the outcome.

If the objective has been achieved, continue to monitor. If the objective has not been achieved, re-run the process. Was the diagnosis correct? Was the objective set properly? Was the correct strategy applied?

If this seems impractically laborious, it isn't. Obviously, the more locations in the chain, the more work to apply the process. Of course, the cost, time, and effort of doing this exercise needs to be compared to the cost, time, and effort of implementing generalized strategies broadly across the chain that are ineffective for many of the locations.

OK, so this all looks straight-forward enough, but I bet applying it is actually a lot more complicated than this framework implies—right? Let's go back to Richard's Sport Shop to see the framework in action.

Richard's Sport Shops: A case study in multi-location performance improvement

When last we left off with Richard, he and his management team just had an epiphany when they saw traffic and conversion rates by location. As we start to apply the performance framework to each location, it's helpful to consider the metrics in the context of the Retail Sales Performance Equation from *Chapter 4* in Figure 7-5. Recall, the formula simply states that Sale Performance is a function of Traffic x Conversion x Average Sale Value.

Starting with Seattle store #2, we see that at 22,130 prospect counts it received the most traffic volume. Average sales conversion at the store was only 28%, which is 7 percentage points below the chain average and 15 percentage points below the top converting store. From an Average Sale perspective, Seattle store #2 was about average at $61.00 per sale.

Based on this data, from a diagnosis perspective, sales conversion appears to be the most obvious area for improvement. If, for example, sales conversion could be increased to 35%, then during this month, based on the 22,130 prospect counts, Seattle store #2 would have done 7,746 sales (*i.e.* 22,130 x .35 = 7,746) instead of the 6,196 it actually did (*i.e.* 22,130 x .28 = 6,196). At a $61.00 average sale, this increase in conversion rate would have generated an incremental $94,495 in revenue (7,746 – 6,196 =1,549 x $61.00 = $94,495).

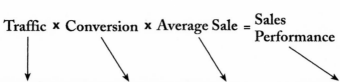

Traffic × Conversion × Average Sale = Sales Performance

Store	Traffic
Seattle #2	22,130
Portland #1	18,350
Seattle #1	15,325
Boise #2	9,120
Portland #2	8,320
Seattle #3	8,300
Spokane	8,125
Great Falls	6,250
Tacoma #1	6,200
Tacoma #2	5,230
Cheyenne	5,225
Boise #1	5,180

Store	Conversion
Boise #1	43%
Tacoma #1	41%
Great Falls	40%
Tacoma #2	38%
Portland #2	38%
Cheyenne	37%
Boise #2	35%
Seattle #3	32%
Spokane	30%
Seattle #2	28%
Seattle #1	27%
Portland #1	25%

Store	Average Sale
Tacoma #1	$72.00
Tacoma #2	$69.00
Boise #1	$68.00
Cheyenne	$67.00
Portland #1	$63.00
Boise #2	$62.00
Great Falls	$62.00
Seattle #2	$61.00
Seattle #3	$60.00
Seattle #1	$58.00
Spokane	$57.00
Portland #2	$56.00

Store	Sales
Seattle #2	$378,000
Portland #1	$289,000
Seattle #1	$240,000
Boise #2	$198,000
Tacoma #1	$183,000
Portland #2	$177,000
Seattle #3	$158,900
Great Falls	$155,000
Boise #1	$151,500
Spokane	$138,900
Tacoma #2	$137,200
Cheyenne	$129,500

Figure 7-5

Table 7-8

Performance metrics — Seattle #2

Store	Traffic
Seattle #2	**22,130**
Portland #1	18,350
Seattle #1	15,325
Boise #2	9,120
Portland #2	8,320
Seattle #3	8,300
Spokane	8,125
Great Falls	6,250
Tacoma #1	6,200
Tacoma #2	5,230
Cheyenne	5,225
Boise #1	5,180

Store	Conversion
Boise #1	43%
Tacoma #1	41%
Great Falls	40%
Tacoma #2	38%
Portland #2	38%
Cheyenne	37%
Boise #2	35%
Seattle #3	32%
Spokane	30%
Seattle #2	**28%**
Seattle #1	27%
Portland #1	25%

Store	Average Sale
Tacoma #1	$72.00
Tacoma #2	$69.00
Boise #1	$68.00
Cheyenne	$67.00
Portland #1	$63.00
Boise #2	$62.00
Great Falls	$62.00
Seattle #2	**$61.00**
Seattle #3	$60.00
Seattle #1	$58.00
Spokane	$57.00
Portland #2	$56.00

Store	Sales
Seattle #2	**$378,000**
Portland #1	$289,000
Seattle #1	$240,000
Boise #2	$198,000
Tacoma #1	$183,000
Portland #2	$177,000
Seattle #3	$158,900
Great Falls	$155,000
Boise #1	$151,500
Spokane	$138,900
Tacoma #2	$137,200
Cheyenne	$129,500

Now that management has diagnosed the most likely performance issue, they need to set a performance target. In this case, because the chain average is 35%, we'll use this as the target conversion rate. So far so good. The tougher question is how do you increase conversion? You might want to review the list of factors that influence conversion rates from *Chapter 4*. With a low conversion rate and a so-so Average Sale per Customer, Richard and his team concluded that the most likely way to drive conversion in Seattle store #2 is through some focused sales training—not only might this help get conversion rates up, but it probably wouldn't hurt the Average Sale per Customer metric either.

Now before Richard and his team start trying to fix Seattle store #2, they need to conduct the same exercise for each location. Let's review two more examples.

Tacoma store #1 was a middle-of-the-pack performer from a sales revenue standpoint, but it had the highest average sale and second highest conversion rate. Impressive. Unfortunately, Tacoma store #1 was in the bottom third in terms of traffic. Given how effective Tacoma store #1 is at converting and given the high average sale value, the trick to driving sales performance simply may be to drive more traffic into the store.

Table 7-9

Performance metrics — Tacoma #1

Store	Traffic	Store	Conver-sion	Store	Average Sale	Store	Sales
Seattle #2	22,130	Boise #1	43%	Tacoma #1	$ 72.00	Seattle #2	$378,000
Portland #1	18,350	Tacoma #1	41%	Tacoma #2	$ 69.00	Portland #1	$289,000
Seattle #1	15,325	Great Falls	40%	Boise #1	$ 68.00	Seattle #1	$240,000
Boise #2	9,120	Tacoma #2	38%	Cheyenne	$ 67.00	Boise #2	$198,000
Portland #2	8,320	Portland #2	38%	Portland #1	$ 63.00	Tacoma #1	$183,000
Seattle #3	8,300	Cheyenne	37%	Boise #2	$ 62.00	Portland #2	$177,000
Spokane	8,125	Boise #2	35%	Great Falls	$ 62.00	Seattle #3	$158,900
Great Falls	6,250	Seattle #3	32%	Seattle #2	$ 61.00	Great Falls	$155,000
Tacoma #1	6,200	Spokane	30%	Seattle #3	$ 60.00	Boise #1	$151,500
Tacoma #2	5,230	Seattle #2	28%	Seattle #1	$ 58.00	Spokane	$138,900
Cheyenne	5,225	Seattle #1	27%	Spokane	$ 57.00	Tacoma #2	$137,200
Boise #1	5,180	Portland #1	25%	Portland #2	$ 56.00	Cheyenne	$129,500

By focusing some marketing effort on the Tacoma area (*e.g.* additional flyer drops or other marketing activities), the imperative here is to drive additional traffic into the location. Assuming Tacoma store #1 can maintain a 41% conversion rate, if prospect traffic for the month could be increased by 15% to about 7,130 prospects (*i.e.* 6,200 x 1.15 = 7,130), this could have a material impact on sales.

So, if Richard and his team can come up with a strategy to drive an incremental 15% more traffic into the Tacoma store #1, assuming the Average Sale per Customer stays constant at $72.00, then the store would generate an additional $27,454 in sales revenue (*i.e.* 7,130 − 6,200 =930 x .41 x $72 = $27,454).

So, for Seattle store #2, the imperative is sales conversion and for Tacoma store #1 it is traffic generation. OK, let's look at one more location. Let's look at Portland store #2.

Portland store #2 consistently has the lowest average sale value in the chain. As the table shows, Portland store #2 is a middle-of-the-pack sales revenue performer, it has a decent amount of traffic and fairly strong sales conversion at 38%. If only Portland store #2 could get their average sales value up, they could generate even more revenue.

Table 7-10

Performance metrics — Portland #2

Store	Traffic	Store	Conversion	Store	Average Sale	Store	Sales
Seattle #2	22,130	Boise #1	43%	Tacoma #1	$ 72.00	Seattle #2	$378,000
Portland #1	18,350	Tacoma #1	41%	Tacoma #2	$ 69.00	Portland #1	$289,000
Seattle #1	15,325	Great Falls	40%	Boise #1	$ 68.00	Seattle #1	$240,000
Boise #2	9,120	Tacoma #2	38%	Cheyenne	$ 67.00	Boise #2	$198,000
Portland #2	**8,320**	**Portland #2**	**38%**	Portland #1	$ 63.00	Tacoma #1	$183,000
Seattle #3	8,300	Cheyenne	37%	Boise #2	$ 62.00	**Portland #2**	**$177,000**
Spokane	8,125	Boise #2	35%	Great Falls	$ 62.00	Seattle #3	$158,900
Great Falls	6,250	Seattle #3	32%	Seattle #2	$ 61.00	Great Falls	$155,000
Tacoma #1	6,200	Spokane	30%	Seattle #3	$ 60.00	Boise #1	$1,500
Tacoma #2	5,230	Seattle #2	28%	Seattle #1	$ 58.00	Spokane	$138,900
Cheyenne	5,225	Seattle #1	27%	Spokane	$ 57.00	Tacoma #2	$137,200
Boise #1	5,180	Portland #1	25%	**Portland #2**	**$ 56.00**	Cheyenne	$129,500

In this case, management needs to focus on increasing the average sale value—perhaps additional sales training is required, perhaps a staff change? If Portland store #2 could increase their average sale from the current $56.00 to $63.00 (about the chain-wide average), assuming that their traffic volume and conversion rate stay constant, they would generate an incremental $22,131 in revenue (8,320 x .38 x ($63-$56) = $22,131).

As these three examples show, the challenge and potential solution can, and likely will, vary by location. Applying a strategy like "drive

Table 7-11

Objective, strategy and incremental revenue target by store

Store	Objective	Strategy	Target Revenue
Boise #1	Drive Traffic	Advertising	$40,000
Boise #2	Increase Conversion	Increase staffing levels	$34,000
Cheyenne	Drive Traffic	Direct mail to existing customers	$34,000
Great Falls	Drive Traffic	Advertising	$46,500
Portland #1	Increase Conversion	Sales Training	$65,000
Portland #2	Increase Average Sale	Sales Training	$27,500
Seattle #1	Increase Conversion	Increase staffing levels	$85,000
Seattle #2	Increase Conversion	Sales Training	$95,000
Seattle #3	Increase Average Sale	Sales Training	$40,000
Spokane	Increase Conversion	Increase staffing levels	$32,000
Tacoma #1	Drive Traffic	Advertising	$55,000
Tacoma #2	Drive Traffic	Advertising	$41,000
Potential Incremental Revenue			**$595,000**

more traffic" broadly across the Richard's Sport Shop chain would not likely be effective in 2 out of the 3 locations!

The Table 7-11 is a summary of management's assessment of the objectives, proposed strategy and expected revenue improvement. As this example shows, Richard and his team just identified a potential incremental $595,000 in sales revenue!

While there are no shortcuts in multi-location performance analysis, that doesn't mean there aren't any economies either. As Table 7-11 shows, several locations have the same objective and performance

Table 7-12

Objective, strategy and incremental revenue target by store

Store	Objective	Strategy	Target Revenue
Boise #1	Drive Traffic	Advertising	$40,000
Cheyenne	Drive Traffic	Direct mail to existing customers	$34,000
Great Falls	Drive Traffic	Advertising	$46,500
Tacoma #1	Drive Traffic	Advertising	$55,000
Tacoma #2	Drive Traffic	Advertising	$41,000
Portland #2	Increase Average Sale	Sales Training	$27,500
Seattle #3	Increase Average Sale	Sales Training	$40,000
Boise #2	Increase Conversion	Increase staffing levels	$34,000
Portland #1	Increase Conversion	Sales Training	$65,000
Seattle #1	Increase Conversion	Increase staffing levels	$85,000
Seattle #2	Increase Conversion	Sales Training	$95,000
Spokane	Increase Conversion	Increase staffing levels	$32,000
Potential Incremental Revenue			$595,000

strategies identified. If we categorize stores with similar objectives and similar performance improvement strategies as in Table 7-12 and Table 7-13 respectively, the whole idea of managing the process and executing across the chain becomes significantly less daunting.

Table 7-13

Potential Incremental Revenue

Store	Objective	Strategy	Target Revenue
Boise #1	Drive Traffic	Advertising	$40,000
Great Falls	Drive Traffic	Advertising	$46,500
Tacoma #1	Drive Traffic	Advertising	$55,000
Tacoma #2	Drive Traffic	Advertising	$41,000
Cheyenne	Drive Traffic	Direct mail to existing customers	$34,000
Boise #2	Increase Conversion	Increase staffing levels	$34,000
Seattle #1	Increase Conversion	Increase staffing levels	$85,000
Spokane	Increase Conversion	Increase staffing levels	$32,000
Portland #2	Increase Average Sale	Sales Training	$27,500
Seattle #3	Increase Average Sale	Sales Training	$40,000
Portland #1	Increase Conversion	Sales Training	$65,000
Seattle #2	Increase Conversion	Sales Training	$95,000
Potential incremental Revenue			$595,000

In fact, now that it's clear what the objectives and strategies are for each store, stores with similar objectives and performance strategies can be grouped. Now Richard's management team can divide and conquer—let the sales manager focus on the sales conversion, have the marketing manager focus on the traffic stimulation initiatives, and so on.

Performance management: The large chain challenge

I am sure some of the readers are thinking "Hey, this approach might be fine and dandy if you have a small chain with similar stores, but if you have a mix of store sizes, store types and even store banners, in a couple of hundred store chain, it's a lot more complicated." You're right. It is more complicated. But of course, the potential benefit from doing it can also be extremely significant. Managers working in very large chains (100 or more locations), need to go through essentially the exact same process in order to understand the performance opportunities at store level. Think of it this way, in a 200 location chain, there might be 5 or 6 regional managers who are each responsible for 30 to 40 stores. These regional managers could lead the effort to review performance for the stores as we did in the Richard's Sport Shop example. Then, it could be rolled-up to provide executive management with a complete summary view as shown in Figure 7-6.

In many ways, applying the performance improvement framework for each location and summarizing the objectives and strategies for all the sites is the easier part. The trickier part can be in bringing the objectives and strategies from all the regions together so that the objectives and strategies can be further grouped, this time across regions. In order to manage the process across the entire organization in an effective way, management will need to take the input from the regional managers and review it in a broader context. Specifically, head office will need to:

- **Review performance**

    First and foremost, senior management will want to understand store level performance. To an extent, this information is nicely contained in the summarized performance matrix that each region has prepared. Senior management may require some additional context that each regional manager should be able to provide.

Performance improvement process across a large chain

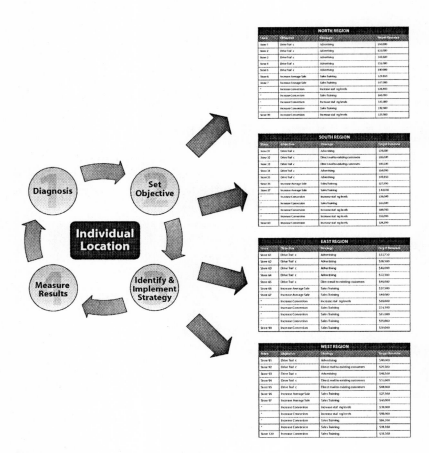

Figure 7-6

• Refine objectives

Although the regional managers working with their store managers have already provided suggested objectives, senior management may want some input on these. For example, the Western Region Manager may have set 35% as the sales conversion target for his stores, but senior management might think 40% is a more appropriate target in light of the performance from the other regions.

- **Review strategies**

As with objectives, senior management may have some thoughts on what the best strategies for driving performance are, based on the stated objectives. Furthermore, senior management will be thinking about the implementation challenges of the respective strategies; naturally they're thinking about strategies across 120 stores, not just the 30 or 40 that the regional manager is concerned about.

- **Prioritize strategies**

Although some strategies may require very little actual investment—in fact, some strategies may only require a change in an internal policy—by and large, driving more traffic through advertising or improving sales conversion through sales training costs money. When you consider the costs of these types of initiatives in a 120 store chain, the investment can be very significant—hundreds of thousands and even millions of dollars. Like any material financial investment, likely senior management will need to prioritize the opportunities. Everything on the list may not get done— at least not right away—but at least it would be a conscious decision by management.

- **Test programs**

As just mentioned, the performance improvement strategies will likely cost money—maybe lots of money. Not only does it make sense to prioritize the performance strategies, it also makes sense to test the strategies first to see if, indeed, the outcome is as expected. For example, before the chain rolls out a comprehensive sales training program (for those locations that need it), management may want to test the training in a few locations (likely in various regions) to see what the results show. If the desired outcomes are achieved, great! If the results are less than expected, maybe some further refinements are needed. Or, perhaps there are several potential sales training companies that need to be evaluated. Perhaps senior management might want to test several training companies by having each do a select number of stores.

• **Formalize implementation plans**

Once the priorities are established and senior management is aligned on which performance strategies will be implemented, detailed implementation plans need to be developed. At this point, the task of implementation is likely pushed back down the organization—senior management has better things to do! Outside vendors or suppliers may need to be contracted, and project plans need to organize such details as timing and scheduling, internal communications, and so on.

• **Roll out programs**

Once it's all done on paper, sleeves need to be rolled up and the work begins. The best laid plans can all be for naught if the programs are not executed well. It all starts with good communications—employees at all levels are more likely to "go with the program" if they understand what the company is trying to accomplish and why.

• **Monitor results**

As a process, this really never ends. Everything changes over time, so management at all levels needs to continue to monitor performance and drive sales results. Very likely, management already has some form of reporting processes in place. Adding traffic and sales conversion metrics to the list would be well advised.

• **Refine as needed**

Not everything will work in all locations the same way. Management needs to create a mechanism for refining programs as needed. If results are not being achieved in a particular location, it could be that the original diagnosis may have been incorrect. Some flexibility is a good thing; however program development "on the fly" is usually not such a good idea. Management needs to find the right balance.

OK, so there is A LOT MORE work to do in a large chain. It's true. The entire process is illustrated in Figure 7-7. But, as previously stated, it's worth it. The fact is, retail managers already spend a great deal of time and energy trying to drive sales performance—they're already doing it! Simply put, if they follow the process just detailed, they will do it more effectively. Think about it, if a small chain like Richard's Sport Shop can identify over $500,000 in potential incremental sales revenue, what do you think a 120 store national chain could find?

**Performance improvement process
across a large chain with Head Office feedback**

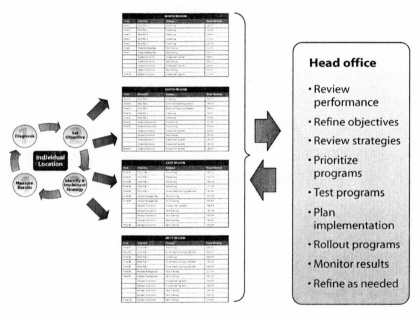

Figure 7-7

Multi-location performance comparisons

There is a tendency in all organizations to compare and rank stores. Ultimately, each location is unique. Even stores with similar physical site characteristics and in the same market can have different, sometimes very different, results. As the previous section showed in great detail, it is imperative for management to understand the performance issues and opportunities of each location individually.

That all said, it is potentially insightful to compare stores. The fact is, chains do it anyway—usually based on sales revenue alone. Why not compare stores on the basis of traffic and sales conversion as well? Although each store is indeed unique, comparing stores based on traffic and conversion rates may offer clues to driving performance that could be used at other stores in the chain. Here is a summary of some of the ways managers might want to compare stores:

- **Market versus market**

  Comparing performance among stores from different geographic regions may provide important insights that can be used to refine programs, and potentially save some cost. For example, a chain of men's wear stores in major cities across the country may observe that traffic spikes 20% on average, the day a sales flyer drops in the New York market, while traffic hardly increases at all in Houston. By comparing traffic responses by market, the marketing department may acquire critical insights that could lead to refinements in media mix, messaging or other promotional elements. It could help them find the secret to spiking traffic in Houston!

- **Format versus format**

  As previously noted, stores in a chain are not necessarily all the same. A chain may have several formats of store—even several formats all in the same geographic market. For example, a bicycle retailer may have two superstores and four standard strip plaza locations all located in Phoenix. The superstores have five times the retail selling space, carry a significantly broader range of products, and have a complete service area. The smaller, strip plaza locations carry only a limited product offering and do not have a service department. Although it's quite obvious that the traffic volume will be different between these two formats, how do they compare on a sales conversion basis? Understanding the differences between the format types provides management with a way of predicting outcomes.

- **Banner versus banner**

  Some chains have multiple banners within their chain organization. For all intents and purposes, to customers, these are different chains. Comparing performance metrics between different brands, like format comparisons, provides management with important clues about the differences in customer behavior in these stores. Understanding customer behavior can help management with formulating and refining strategies to drive performance.

- **Store versus store**

Lastly, some chains strive for consistency in look and feel across the entire chain. In this case, these chains usually employ a national advertising program, merchandising programs, and sales training—basically, everything. The temptation to compare these stores is strong, and why shouldn't it be? To a large extent they are comparable. As we saw in the Richard's Sport Shop example, management's view of what good performance is can change when they look at more than just sales revenue as a performance measure.

Comparing store performance is a natural and important way for management to understand what's happening and potentially how it's happening. Although management can, and should, compare stores—on lots of dimensions including those just listed—it is also important that management understands that there may be good reasons why one location consistently out performs another location. For example, one of the stores may be located right beside a major competitor; clearly this will impact performance, and management needs to keep this in mind.

Lastly, management needs to consider how these comparisons will be interpreted by store level managers. As the next section will show, it can get personal.

The pitfalls of performance comparisons

A discussion I had with a manager of a consumer electronics retail store some years ago nicely illustrates some of the potential dynamics of performance comparisons that management needs to be sensitive to. The conversation went something like this:

> **Author**: "It's great that you're measuring traffic now so that you can calculate sales conversion rates."

Store Manager: "Yes, it sure is. I think this is going to be very useful."

Author: "Let me ask you, your company has a store on the south side of town as well, right?"

Store Manager: "Right."

Author: "Do you think the manager of your south side store would be interested in hearing about traffic counting and conversion rates?"

Store Manager: (half-laughing) "Are you kidding me?"

Author: "No, why not?"

Store Manager: "Our south side store probably gets twice as much traffic as I do here downtown. His sales volume is only slightly higher than mine. In fact, occasionally, I actually have higher sales. I don't think it's in his best interest to track it."

Author: "I suspect that head office might feel differently about it."

I'm not suggesting that retail store managers are all self-interested, conniving, Machiavellians out to mislead head office—on the contrary. I think the example above is probably a special case, though it can happen. There is a natural tendency to want to present one's performance in the most positive light possible, and retail managers are not exempt from this tendency.

Generally, most store managers truly want to drive performance in their stores. They do want to be the best they can be. That said, this isn't always the case. As I found out, not all managers may find it personally beneficial for head office to break their performance down into its constituent components. "Hey, sales are going up, so what's the problem?"

As explained in *Chapter 4* on sales conversion, sales revenue alone is problematic because it fails to provide any perspective on what the potential opportunity is—in many ways this is far more useful in measuring store (and the store managers') performance. The store that captures more of the opportunity is a better performer than a store that captures less, even if the store that captures less of the opportunity actually has higher sales. Think of it this way, how much more successful would you be if you had your best store manager running every location? That's what this is about.

Whose job is it anyway?

When it comes to managing the traffic data in a large chain, you might think it would be easier to identify the person who has responsibility than in a small chain. The fact is, it's less obvious. Because there are so many potential stakeholders for the traffic information, it tends to get lost in the organization. We have seen countless examples of large, sophisticated retail chains that can't point us to the "owner" of the traffic information. Unfortunately, traffic data is often not readily or reliably available.

It is irrelevant who owns the traffic information, as long as there is an owner. Designate someone—anyone! The traffic "function" could quite nicely fit in Marketing or Store Operations. We have seen it in Information Systems, even Finance. Wherever it ends up, as long as someone is responsible for the traffic information and ensures that all the stakeholders have ample access, the company will be in good shape.

Chapter Summary

- Traffic analysis is critical to any retailer, but it's even more critical to multi-location chains. The type of chain organization can have an impact on how complicated the traffic analysis will be. Traffic analysis complexity generally goes up with the number of stores and markets the chain does business in—from local to regional to national chains. Other characteristics, like the number of different store formats in a chain and the number of different banners, will also increase complexity.

- There are many stakeholders of traffic data in a chain operation. From store level managers, to regional managers, to head office marketing, sales, operations, and even the executive management, the need for, and potential uses of, traffic information are many within a chain operation.

- One of the most important uses of the traffic information in a chain is as an input for performance metrics. As discussed in *Chapter 4* on sales conversion, without traffic data, there is no way to calculate sales conversion rates—and sales conversion is the fundamental measure that every retailer needs to understand. When good performance metrics have been established, it's important that management resist the temptation to apply one solution generally across the entire chain. Management needs to understand what the most likely performance drivers are for each location, categorize the performance improvement strategies and move to implementation. This on-going process will enable management to drive continuous improvement across the chain.

- Comparing performance across a chain can be tricky. Variations in market, store format, banner and even subtle differences among stores with similar characteristics can make inter-store comparisons somewhat problematic. Also, performance comparisons can be distracting for the store managers.

- Lastly, chain organizations need to designate someone as the traffic information owner. It is of little use to collect traffic data if it is not used regularly or broadly across the organization.

Web, Phone and Store Traffic
The Complete Picture

The majority of retailers today offer products through multiple sales channels; in order to understand the complete traffic picture, retailers need to track traffic in all channels.

Web, Phone and Store Traffic

WHEN WE THINK OF RETAIL TODAY, we rarely confine the definition to only bricks and mortar physical locations. Retail has been evolving and changing over the past decade in particular, as retailers in virtually every category look for new and creative ways to make their products available to customers.

The advent of cost effective, toll-free telephone was a logical extension to the catalogers and mail order houses—many of whom also started out with physical stores.

WEB, PHONE, STORE

- How retailers retail
- All sources
- Measuring ad performance
- Sales conversion analysis
- Traffic dashboard

Of course, during the mid-90s the promise of global retailing had retailers of every size and shape scurrying to get their wares on the Internet. Web stores were considered a huge threat to traditional retailing, with some pundits and technology gurus predicting the end of retailing as we know it—bye-bye bricks and mortar and hello Web store.

Ten years later, here we are. Notwithstanding the pure-play Web retailers like Amazon.com and DELL, many traditional retailers find their Web stores to be a nice complement to their existing business, but retail certainly hasn't gone away as some had predicted. To a large extent, traditional retailers still rely on people visiting their stores to buy.

In this chapter, we will examine the impact of the Internet and telephone on retail traffic analysis and how, for retailers who employ them, these channels should be incorporated into traffic analysis in order to provide a complete picture of performance and to measure results.

How retailers retail today

According to a recent Gardner Consulting survey of 375 US and European retailers, 75% of respondents either had a multi-channel retailing strategy or were planning one. In Canada, the figures are similar. According to *The Canadian Retail Technology Survey* conducted by the Retail Council of Canada in conjunction with the J.C. Williams Group, virtually all retailers surveyed said they were embracing a multi-channel strategy, with approximately 90% either having or planning to have a website.

The fact is, there are very few retailers today who don't use the telephone or Internet as part of their operation in some way—either to sell products outright or to support the sale of these items in-store.

Before we delve into the traffic implications of these channels, let's look at them in a little more detail starting with the Web.

Web retailing: A brief overview

Interestingly, in some ways, the Internet craze focused attention on traffic counting. In fact, one of the key metrics bandied-about during the 90s was hits or Web traffic. Actually, it still is an important metric today. These Web people understood the importance of counting traffic from the beginning! Of course, traffic in a physical brick and mortar retail store is the equivalent of hits on a Web store. Just as the Web retailers needed to understand hits, so do brick and mortar retailers. Let's look at some of the characteristics of Web stores as they relate to their physical counterparts.

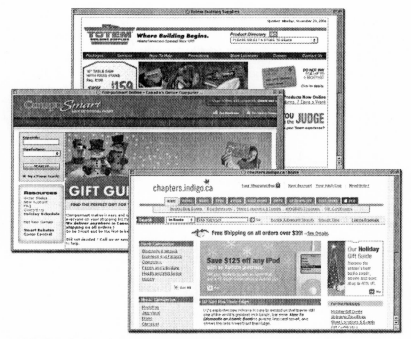

© TOTEM Building Supplies Ltd, Copyright ©2004 Hartco Corporation and
Copyright © Indigo Books & Music Ltd.

Figure 8-1

Web store versus "Brochure ware"

The impact of a retailer's website on traffic analysis will depend
greatly upon what type of website they have. In very general terms,
we can break retail websites into two groups:

1. selling and

2. non-selling sites.

Selling sites

As the name suggests, these retail websites not only offer products
for sale, but actually enable customers to purchase or order the product online. Sometimes referred to as "e-commerce" or Web stores,
these websites are designed to sell products. Customers can browse
the store, select products, place the items they wish to purchase in
their virtual shopping cart and check out. As part of the process,

customers pay for their purchase using a credit card, or some other form of electronic payment, and then their purchase is sent to them by mail or courier.

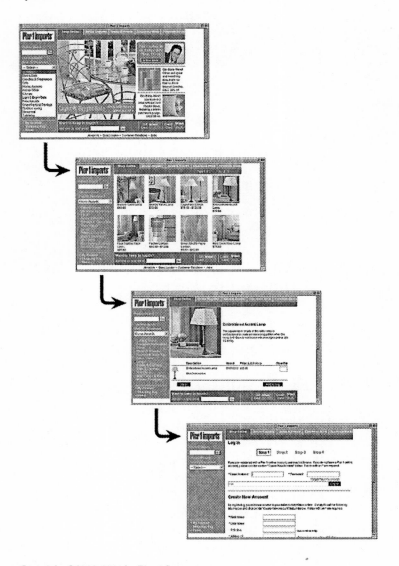

Copyright ©2002-2004 by Pier 1 Imports

Figure 8-2

Non-selling sites

Sometimes affectionately referred to as "brochure ware," these retail sites do not have a Web store component. Prospects can usually find information on product offerings, sometimes even detailed specifications and pictures, but they cannot actually buy or order the products. Even though they don't actually sell product on these websites, retailers may create them for a variety of good reasons:

- **To establish a Web presence**

   Given the Internet boom of the 90s, retailers couldn't afford not to have a Web presence. In many ways, retailers who didn't have websites (selling or non-selling), were considered old-fashioned, and some thought that they would be missing an important and new market if they didn't have a website. Publicly traded retailers were especially pressured as stockholders, believing that Web retailing was the future, would label the retailer as un-progressive. Even if the retailers' product offering didn't lend itself to online selling, it was in the retailer's best interest to build a website—even a brochure ware site—and many did just that.

- **To provide important product information**

   Even though the retailer isn't selling his products online, for

Figure 8-3

some retailers it is still useful to post detailed product information. For example, by their very nature, auto dealers need prospects to visit their showrooms to buy a vehicle; however, providing prospects with detailed product information on their website can be a great way to help customers get the information they need to make a purchase. This is especially useful for high involvement or complex purchase decisions.

- **To pre-sell prospects**

  Arming prospects with product information is a great way to pre-sell prospects. When people are informed, especially for high-involvement or complex purchases, sales conversion rates can be positively impacted. For example, if a prospect is considering buying a bed mattress, they may want to look at all the alternatives and read about the latest in mattress technology. With a good information site, a prospect can essentially select their purchase. When they ultimately visit the store to see the actual product, to an extent they are already pre-disposed to purchase. They ask informed questions, and have moved themselves further along in the sales cycle compared to, say, a person who walks into a mattress store for the first time and needs to engage a salesperson to answer a bunch of pre-sale questions.

- **To provide other important information**

  Whether retailers have a Web store or not, the Internet has proven to be an invaluable resource for consumers. In addition to using the Web to get specific product information, many retail websites offer a wide range of information that consumers would find useful, like store hours, store addresses and telephone numbers, company background, awards, community involvement, and even employment opportunities. Regardless of whether a retailer offers products directly for sale on their website or not, a website is an important retailing tool.

Web retailing: Final thoughts

Notwithstanding the hype of the 90s, the Internet has been good for retail. With the Internet, retailers can offer 24 hour access to prospects—something that just isn't practical in traditional bricks

©2004 Sleep Country Canada

Figure 8-4

and mortar retailing. Furthermore, the Internet enables retailers to showcase themselves and their product offerings in ways that just weren't previously possible. The cost and effort required to build and maintain a website have significantly decreased, making the Internet a must-have for all retailers.

As much as websites are a critical part of retailing today—both selling and non-selling sites—there are certain things websites just can't do. Despite great efforts by Web developers to make websites interactive and intuitive, there is no substitute for a real, thinking, breathing human being to help with a purchase decision. We will now have a quick look at telephone retailing before we get into the nitty-gritty of traffic analysis.

Catalog and telephone retailing:
The predecessor of the Web

Decades before the Internet became the Internet, retailers were looking for ways to expand their market—to reach more customers and increase convenience. Mailing out catalogs and other sales literature, and having customers phone or mail in their orders, was a good way to do this. As the cost of long distance rates dropped, and the ease of securing a toll-free line became practical, retailers began to embrace the telephone as an additional and important sales channel.

Obviously, telephone sales enable retailers to interact with prospects directly. Like in-store staff, telephone sales representatives can assist the customer with their purchases—make recommendations, make add-on sales and answer questions in real-time. Some prospects need and want the human interaction before making a purchase.

Again, depending upon the product offering, retailers may or may not offer catalog or telephone sales as part of their business. In some segments, like office supplies and consumer electronics, catalog and telephone sales are important channels; other segments, like furniture and clothing, tend to be less so.

Retail traffic analysis is not *just* about the volume and timing of prospects that walk into the store. When prospects visit a retailer's website, they create "web traffic." When customers phone a retailer they create "phone traffic." In order to get a complete picture on advertising effectiveness and sales conversion, retailers need to combine these traffic sources in order to get the complete understanding of what's happening—and that's exactly what we'll turn to next.

Traffic analysis—all sources

Now that we have defined the additional sources of traffic (Web and telephone), we need to consider how they should be factored into our traffic analysis. The fact is, readers could virtually re-read the entire book replacing "store traffic" with "Web traffic" and "telephone traffic." For example, just as staff planning in the store could be optimized by analyzing traffic patterns, retailers with call centers will need to understand call volume and timing to plan operator staffing. Understanding the number of hits and transactions on the retailer's website will provide the retailer with critical information about the staffing needs of the website—in this case, it usually translates into the number and capacity of Web servers or technology infrastructure supporting the website.

Although we'll leave most of the review to the readers, we will focus on two key areas of traffic analysis that should be well understood:

1. measuring the impact of advertising and

2. sales conversion.

Measuring advertising performance

Until this chapter, we have basically assumed that retail traffic meant prospects physically visiting a store. More specifically, we have assumed that *the* advertising objective is to increase the number of qualified prospects that visit your store. OK, so far so good. But here's the question—what should your objective be if you also have a Web store or call center?

If you have a Web store and you offer prospects the ability to "shop-by-phone," you will need to account for these sources of traffic in your advertising response measure. The objective may be no longer *just* to drive prospect traffic into the physical store.

Call-to-action—what are you asking prospects to do?

All effective advertising includes a "call-to-action." A call-to-action is simply a response request—it's a statement that asks that prospects do something—visit the store, call the toll-free number, visit a website. The call-to-action may be specific and literal ("shop today and save") or it might be implied. That is, the advertisement may not specifically say do something today but by the virtue of featuring "loss leader" products, using the word SALE and including store hours and location information, the implication is that the retailer is asking prospects to visit.

Measuring the impact of advertising is essentially measuring the reaction to the call-to-action. If you ask customers to "visit the store and save" or "shop our complete selection of mattresses online" or "call to order—shipping is free," you are asking customers to visit the store, call or point their Web browsers to your website. In each case, you should expect to see some measurable response to this request. If you don't get a measurable response, then something went wrong; as was discussed in *Chapter 1*, there could be countless factors that led to the lack of response, and you'll need to do a little digging and experimenting to figure out why. On the other hand, if you get a positive (*i.e.* increased) traffic response—hooray, your advertising worked (this time).

The ad sample in Figure 8-5 illustrates a case in which prospects have three ways to shop. If retailers who have multiple sales channels only measured prospect traffic in their stores, they would not have a complete picture on how their advertising performed. For example, what if store traffic increased only very modestly? In isolation, the marketing manager might conclude that the advertising was ineffective. But what if Web traffic and incoming calls to the call center increased dramatically? Obviously, this would lead to a different conclusion.

Copyright ©2004 The Business Depot

Figure 8-5

Let's look at the idea of measuring advertising response with multiple traffic response sources using Richard's Sport Shops as an example.

Richard's Sport Shop: Spring Sales Event

For four days in early March, every March, Richard and his team kick off the season by holding a major sales event. In fact, it's the

Figure 8-6

first big event of the year. Superstitiously, Richard views this sales event as the bellwether for the coming year—"if we have a strong March sale, I know it's going to be a good year."

Richard's Sport Shops offers products in-store, online at richardsportshop.com or by phone. As a matter of policy, Richard ensures that every advertisement includes store hours, addresses, the Web address and, of course, the telephone number. As Richard says, "I just don't understand retailers who make it hard for customers—why wouldn't you make all your contact information really easy to find and read in your ads?"

For this March sale, an 8-page color flyer was inserted into the daily newspaper on March 9th and reminder support advertisements ran in the newspaper on March 10th and 11th, as shown in Figure 8-6.

Naturally when the promotion kicked-off, Richard and his team were anxiously waiting to see the results.

- **Store traffic**

    As the chart in Figure 8-7 shows, store traffic during the promotion was up over 33% compared to the period prior to the promotion, and up 28% compared to traffic levels

Store traffic by day

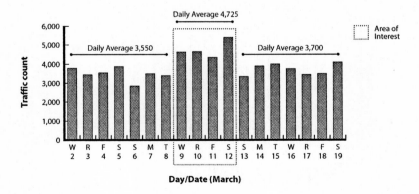

Figure 8-7

after the promotion. The busiest day during the promotion occurred on Saturday March 12th. Based on store traffic, Richard should be quite pleased with the result—there was a material increase in traffic during his promotion. Furthermore, year-over-year traffic for the same promotional period was up by a healthy 18%.

- **Web traffic**

Although Richard still prefers to sell products the good old-fashioned, face-to-face way, he can't deny the impact his Web store has had on business. With his Web store, Richard can reach customers from across North America and beyond. During the promotion, Web store traffic is shown in the chart in Figure 8-8. Like store traffic, Web traffic spiked significantly during the promotion. The average daily hits to Richard's website almost doubled during the promotional period and then, like store traffic, dropped back to more normal levels after the sales event.

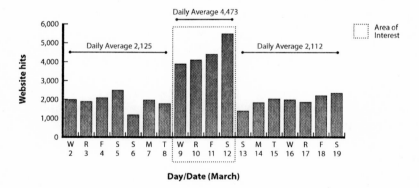

Figure 8-8

- **Phone traffic**

As the chart in Figure 8-9 shows, the number of telephone calls received by Richard's Sport Shops was actually *down* during the promotion, compared to the periods both before the promotion and after. Year-over-year phone traffic wasn't much better at -10%. Clearly prospects weren't calling to place orders like they used to.

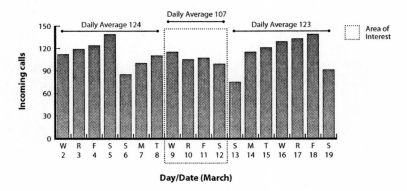

Calls received by day

Figure 8-9

By looking at the traffic response for each traffic source, management can get a clearer understanding of what the total traffic response to advertising or the promotion is. In this case, it's clear that the advertising generated a positive traffic response in the store and on the Web, but call volumes were down.

Although it is vital to understand traffic response in order to measure advertising effectiveness, to an extent, management can influence where prospects respond.

Factors influencing the response channel

Although customers will respond to an advertisement in a way that is most convenient for them, there are a number of factors that will influence where, when, and how prospects respond.

• Channel emphasis

If a retailer wanted to drive traffic to his Web store, he might design the advertisement such that the call-to-action strongly favors the Web. For example, "Shop 24 hours a day on the Web at www.mystore.com and get an additional 10% off."

Clearly this retailer is trying to drive traffic to his Web store. Retailers emphasize channel through the specific copy they choose, size of type, incentives, and communication vehicle (*e.g.* an e-mail campaign is likely to drive Web traffic). If a retailer emphasizes "visit the store today" as the primary call-to-action, but also includes a website address and a telephone number, they would expect the biggest traffic response to be in-store with more modest responses on the Web and phone.

- **Product type**

  Naturally the type of products being sold will influence the response channel. For example, although you could browse for furniture over the Internet, before a prospect makes a purchase, very likely they will want to see and feel the actual merchandise. The only way to do this is to visit the store. Likely, high involvement or complex product purchases are not going to be made over the Internet or telephone. That said, prospects could visit the retailer's website to research products or call and ask questions, before they visit the store to buy.

Sales conversion analysis

As with advertising response, it is also useful to measure sales conversion rates by channel. As we've already learned, sales conversion is a critical performance measure, and just as it is important to understand how well you are converting prospects into customers in the store, it is useful to understand how well you're converting on your Web store and on the phone.

In this section we will look at how retailers can measure sales conversion across channels to get a complete picture of sales performance compared to the opportunity.

Calculating conversion rates: Comparing apples to bananas

Just like your physical store, if you sell products on the Web or by phone, they too have a sales conversion rate. And, just as we calculate and measure conversion rates in the store to understand performance versus the opportunity, the same rules apply to the Web and phone—well, sort of.

Although the sales conversion rate can be calculated and compared, there are nuances in conversion among the channels that should be noted.

Web conversion

We'll leave the heavy lifting of Web selling and Web stores to the Internet experts; however, there are a few basics every retailer who offers products on the Web (in addition to their physical store) should understand.

Simply put, Web store conversion is calculated similarly to physical store conversion as follows:

$$\text{Sales Conversion} = \frac{\text{Transactions}}{\text{Website Hits}}$$

(*i.e.* **prospect traffic**)

In this case the website hits represent the store traffic. Part of the trick is to be consistent in how the variables are being used. For example, there are total hits which represent every time a particular Web page is visited—even if it's by the same prospect over and over during the same shopping trip. It would be sort of like a prospect visiting your physical store, and walking in and out of the store throughout the visit—clearly this would drive your traffic counts up and your sales conversion rate down.

The other way to measure conversion, and a better way at that, would be to use unique hits for your website traffic variable. As the name implies, some Web reporting tools can actually tell you how many unique visitors came to your website by tracking the visitor's Internet Protocol (sometimes called the IP address), which is essentially an identifier that distinguishes one visitor from another in a fairly innocuous way. By using unique hits, retailers can get a good idea of how many different people are visiting their site and then calculate a reasonably accurate Web store sales conversion rate.

For example, if Richard's Sport Shop Web store received 2,000 unique hits in a day, and the total number of sales transactions on the site that day was 200, then his Web store conversion rate would be 10%.

$$10\% = \frac{200}{2,000}$$

Factors effecting Web conversion

There are countless great books and guides on Web store design, so we'll leave it to the reader to dig deeper into this topic if they wish, but here are a few basic ideas to keep in mind:

- **Check out**

  Like the line-up at the till, getting online shoppers through your virtual check-out is critical. In fact, research shows that many Internet shoppers abandon their purchase at check-out. That's why Web designers and Web store experts spend so much time thinking about check out. If check out is complicated or confusing, people will just leave. Unlike a physical store where the prospects who drove to your store may be a little more patient (and are almost certainly NOT confused by your check-out process), on the Web, it's as easy as a click of a mouse and they're gone.

- **Web store layout and design**

  Like the physical store, Web stores need to be well designed. The trick is to design a Web store that is easy and intuitive to navigate. Many retailers don't offer their complete product offering on the Web, so decisions about what you choose to show become critical. Also, how graphic intensive the site is can impact performance. For example, websites that use large graphics, or Flash animation/video can be compelling and interesting, but if prospects don't have high-speed Internet access, the site can be so painfully slow that prospects will just leave. Great Web stores take all this into consideration and much more.

- **Customer confidence in e-commerce**

  Although shopping online has become a part of every day life, still many consumers don't feel confident about buying online. Oh, they'll browse around like crazy—researching products, comparing items and looking for the best price, but when it comes time to make the purchase, many consumers will order by phone or visit the store. Although it may be difficult for any given retailer to change consumer perceptions about e-commerce security, there are some things retailers can do to build confidence in their Web store such as securing third party certifications that represent safety and security in e-commerce.

Phone conversion

Like Web conversion, phone conversion is simply calculated by taking the number of sales or transactions made by phone and dividing them by the total number of sales calls; this is the same as hits to your Web store or traffic in your store.

$$\text{Sales Conversion} = \frac{\text{Transactions}}{\text{Telephone Calls}}$$

Factors effecting phone conversion

Like information on Web stores, practical guides and books on call centers and telephone sales are readily available. So, again, we'll leave it to the reader to dig into the topic more if they wish. However, here are a few ideas retailers should keep in mind about telephone sales.

- **Product offering**

  Calling up a retailer to order a box of paper is one thing, but trying to order a complete home theatre package is another. The fact is, some products are just easier to sell by phone (or by Web) than others. Of course, catalogers have been selling products of every imaginable type for years, so it is possible.

- **Hours of operation**

  To an extent, the telephone sales business has created an expectation among consumers that they can call—and someone will answer—virtually any time of the day or night. If you are a traditional bricks and mortar retailer, with traditional bricks and mortar store hours, some prospects might be disappointed if your telephone hours are not longer than your store hours.

- **Staffing levels**

  Staffing levels are even more critical in call centers than in retailer showrooms because of the lack of self-help. When a customer visits your physical store, they may or may not require sales assistance. They might just want to browse the store and self-select items to purchase. In telephone sales, every prospect needs to be attended to—there is no such thing as self-help in telephone sales. Even with sophisticated call routing and automation, eventually that call-in prospect will need to speak with a salesperson. Prospects that call in and can't get through in a reasonable amount of time, will just stop calling.

- **Telephone selling skills**

  Selling skills are critical in retail, period, but to an extent they are even more important in telephone sales. Whereas in a retail store, customers can touch and see the product, by phone (or Web) a picture may be the best they will have. Also, sales people dealing with in-store prospects have a chance to read the body language of prospects; they can get a better sense of how the prospect is reacting to what they are seeing, and consequently, are in a better position to make the sale. Selling by telephone is harder than selling face-to-face, and good telephone sales people have to know the products extremely well, have excellent telephone manners, and understand the nuances of telephone selling.

Creating a complete traffic dashboard

If you are a retailer who has a Web store in addition to telephone sales and a bricks and mortar store, the idea of creating a complete traffic dashboard can seem daunting. And it's true, it can be a lot of work to create it and more importantly keep updated; however, tracking traffic and sales conversion across your different sales channels will provide tremendous insight into what's happening in your business and where. Here is an example of what a traffic dashboard might look like Table 8-1.

As for Richard's Sport Shops, his total traffic might be represented in a chart like Figure 8-10.

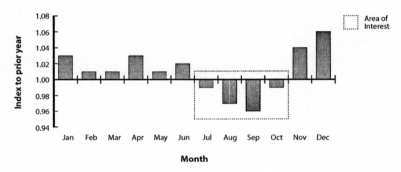

Figure 8-10

Table 8-1

Complete traffic dashboard

	Store Traffic				Website Traffic				Telephone Traffic				Total Traffic (All Sources)		
	Current Month	Index vs. Prior Month	Index vs. Prior Year		Current Month	Index vs. Prior Month	Index vs. Prior Year		Current Month	Index vs. Prior Month	Index vs. Prior Year		Current Month	Index vs. Prior Month	Index vs. Prior Year
Jan	9,000	0.93	1.06	Jan	2,200	0.92	0.99	Jan	166	0.75	1.02	Jan	11,366	0.80	1.03
Feb	11,000	1.22	1.02	Feb	2,500	1.14	1.00	Feb	175	1.05	1.00	Feb	13,675	1.20	1.01
Mar	12,500	1.14	1.01	Mar	2,700	1.08	1.01	Mar	170	0.97	1.02	Mar	15,370	1.12	1.01
Apr	14,800	1.18	1.03	Apr	3,350	1.24	1.00	Apr	198	1.16	1.03	Apr	18,348	1.19	1.03
May	13,500	0.91	1.00	May	5,400	1.61	0.99	May	220	1.11	1.01	May	19,120	1.04	1.01
Jun	15,000	1.11	1.05	Jun	5,750	1.06	1.00	Jun	255	1.16	1.00	Jun	21,005	1.10	1.02
Jul	16,000	1.07	0.98	Jul	6,100	1.06	1.02	Jul	312	1.22	0.99	Jul	22,412	1.07	0.99
Aug	10,100	0.63	0.95	Aug	4,400	0.72	1.01	Aug	190	0.61	0.99	Aug	14,690	0.66	0.97
Sep	8,500	0.84	0.98	Sep	4,000	0.91	1.04	Sep	135	0.71	1.05	Sep	12,635	0.86	0.96
Oct	7,500	0.88	1.00	Oct	3,900	0.98	0.99	Oct	155	1.15	1.00	Oct	11,555	0.91	0.99
Nov	5,600	0.75	1.06	Nov	1,890	0.48	0.98	Nov	100	0.65	1.00	Nov	7,590	0.66	1.04
Dec	11,500	2.05	1.08	Dec	2,400	1.27	1.02	Dec	220	2.20	0.90	Dec	14,120	1.86	1.06

Chapter Summary

- Many retailers today offer prospective buyers more than one way to shop—it's not just about visiting the physical store. As much as it's critical for retailers to understand the volume and timing of prospects visiting their store, it's just as important for retailers to understand "traffic" from the other channels they have. The three primary channels are the store, the Internet and telephone.

- The Internet has changed the face of retail. Many retailers today have some kind of Web presence. Some retailers create websites merely to tell customers about themselves and their offerings without actually selling anything. These brochure ware sites can be very useful for informing prospects about store hours, store locations, directions, special events or sales, and community service or charities that the retailer supports. Even though prospects can't buy on these websites, these sites help predispose prospects to purchase, and compel them to visit the store so they can buy.

- Web stores or full e-commerce websites are websites that customers can actually make purchases from. These websites are designed with buying in mind, and prospects can browse the Web store, select items they wish to purchase, and then actually purchase the items—all online.

- Traffic response to advertising is one area that retailers will want to understand across all three channels. What happens to store, Web and phone traffic during a promotion? By tracking store traffic, Web hits and incoming phone calls, multi-channel retailers can understand what impact their promotions are having. Also, by comparing channels, they can understand how prospects like to shop. One of the key factors in measuring traffic response is to start with the call-to-action. Fundamentally, retailers need to be clear about what they are asking prospects to do, and then try to measure that behavior.

- Sales conversion is another key area of multi-channel retailing that needs to be understood. Just as sales conversion can be calculated in the physical store by dividing transactions by traffic, conversion rates for Web stores and call centers can also be calculated. The factors that influence conversion rates will vary by channel, and retailers need to understand what the conversion drivers are in order to influence them positively.

- In order to understand how the business is performing and changing over time, retailers should create and maintain traffic and sales conversion dashboards that show exactly how traffic levels and sales conversion change over time and among the channels.

CHAPTER

The Strategic Value of Traffic Insights

Just as traffic information has a breadth of uses, it also has a depth of uses—from the part-time store manager to the CEO.

The Strategic Value of Traffic Insights

TRAFFIC INFORMATION, BY AND LARGE, is relegated to the less than high profile bastion of "tactical" management. OK, you can optimize staffing; yes, you can gauge the impact of advertising, and you can calculate conversion rates—great stuff. Traffic analysis is a useful tool for store managers to help them run the store better. But it's not something senior executives need to concern themselves with. After all, senior executives need to focus on the big picture. They need to take a broader, longer term perspective on the business. In short, they need to be "strategic." Traffic data isn't strategic—is it?

STRATEGIC VALUE OF TRAFFIC

- Long-term trends
- Location strategies
- Corporate reporting
- Competitive analysis
- Planning and modeling
- Benchmarking

If strategic is to refer to things that are fundamental to the business, are critical to success, have multiple applications across an entire organization at all levels, and speak to the absolute lifeblood of what a retail business is, then I guess you might say traffic data is strategic. Of course traffic data is strategic! Or, more to the point, traffic data can be used for strategic purposes. From identifying long-term business trends, to corporate reporting, forecasting and benchmarking, traffic information can be used in a myriad of ways for strategic purposes. In this chapter, we will cover some of the most important strategic uses of traffic information.

If you are a small chain retailer or operate only one location, don't skip this chapter—unless, of course, you want to stay small. Small retail operations need to deal with strategic issues just like large retail organizations. You may be small, but you need to think about the long-term. You need to plan and forecast, you need to consider your competition and you may be planning to expand. OK, maybe there are a few areas in this chapter that don't really apply—yet—but most of it will. Keep reading.

Long-term trends

If there is one thing every retailer knows, it is that things are constantly changing. Customers' needs change, the market is changing, the competitive landscape is changing, product offerings change—in short, everything is in a constant state of flux. That's why it is imperative to monitor traffic (and the other measures you currently look at) in order to not only be able to understand what may be happening, but more importantly, in order to influence the outcome. You can't influence the outcome of if you have no idea of where things are going.

Let's start with something every retailer would agree is strategic—sales revenue trends.

Revenue trends

The chart in Figure 9-1 shows the long term sales revenue trend for a retail operation. All things being equal, this is not a bad trend. Yes, of course, we would always like to see revenue increasing, but based on this trend, the company has had pretty good revenue growth over the years. Although the last four years have been a little flat, there doesn't appear to be anything especially alarming about the trend. Of course, the retailer also would be watching margins and profitability along with revenue, but even these additional metrics may not indicate any ominous signs. But by looking at only financial metrics, this retailer just might not have a full understanding of what may be happening in the business.

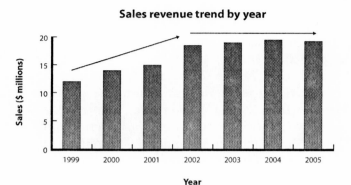

Figure 9-1

Traffic trends

The chart in Figure 9-2 shows the long term traffic trend for the same retailer. As you can see, this retailer had strong traffic growth from 1999 to 2002. After 2002, traffic started to decline. This decline in traffic could have been a result of a number of external or internal factors: competitors, changing customer behavior, changes in marketing spending by the retailer, or a host of other issues. The

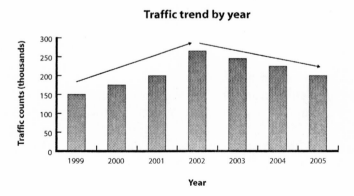

Figure 9-2

point is that the traffic volume has changed. The pattern is clear—since 2002, traffic has steadily decreased at an alarming rate.

Looking at the traffic trend in a year-over-year comparative as shown in Figure 9-3, we see a picture that looks even more disturbing. We can clearly see in the chart, traffic growth rates from 2000 to 2002 ranged from 14% in 2000 to a very healthy 33% in 2002. Starting in 2003, however, things began to change. Traffic in 2003 was down 8% from 2002. OK, no panic yet, after all, 2002 was an exceptional year, right? Unfortunately, the pattern continues. Traffic in 2004 was down another 8% and in 2005 traffic was down 11% from 2004. Think of it this way, traffic levels in 2005 were the same as they were in 2001—4 years earlier!

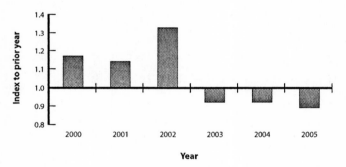

Figure 9-3

Traffic and revenue

When we combine our standard financial metrics with traffic, a more complete picture of the long-term trend becomes clear, as shown in Figure 9-4. Even though revenue builds and flattens out, traffic levels build and then drop. Interestingly, during 2004 and 2005, even though sales revenue is actually growing (albeit very modestly), traffic levels are dropping off significantly.

The only way it is possible for sales to increase while traffic decreases is if:

     1. the average sales value per customer is increasing (because

customers are buying more items per transaction or because the cost of products has increased),

2. sales conversion rates are increasing (*i.e.* the retailer is actually converting more of the prospects that enter the store even though fewer are coming in) or

3. some combination of increased conversion rates and increasing average sales value.

The fact is, if the retailer was only looking at average sale value or sales conversion rates, they might conclude that their performance was actually improving. And, they would be right! If sales conversion rates and/or average sales values are increasing, performance is improving. What's really insidious is that these relatively positive performance metrics mask the fact that this retailer's traffic has consistently declined over the past three years. If I was this retailer, I would be worried. What's going on here? Eventually, conversion rates and average sale values will level out, leaving the retailer scratching his head wondering why his sales performance has stalled. By understanding the long-term traffic patterns, the retailer is in a position to take action on the traffic. If you can increase traffic in addition to increasing average sales value and conversion rates, we know what a powerfully positive impact it can have on sales performance. Furthermore, by recognizing that traffic is declining, the retailer can start to try to understand why—and then do something about it before it becomes a problem.

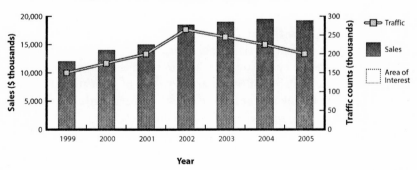

Comparison of annual sales and traffic trends

Figure 9-4

Location strategies

Notwithstanding some very unique or rare situations, retailers open additional stores (or close and move existing stores) in order to generate incremental traffic, and consequently, incremental sales. That's the intention anyway. Unfortunately, that's not always what happens. Location strategy, and the techniques for determining where to locate stores, has developed into a science—however, while some retailers are only doing high school biology, others are lecturing PhDs! Sophisticated population modeling, demographic profiling, and geographic information systems are proving to be important tools, but not every retail organization has the time, energy, and resources to put these techniques to use.

Having an understanding of traffic patterns and volumes can be very helpful in location decisions and strategy. Not only can traffic be used to help identify potential locations for new stores, but it can also provide invaluable insight into the impact of the decision on existing locations—was it a good decision are not?

New markets

Obviously, when a retailer decides to open a new store in a new market (*i.e.* a market where they don't already have a store), there is no risk of cannibalizing traffic or sales from a current location. By analyzing traffic patterns and volume from existing stores with similar characteristics as the new proposed store, management can get important clues about what to look for in the ideal location. For example, if a retailer knows that, based on current store performance, the type of location that received the most traffic is a free standing building located within close proximity to a major retail "power center," then the retailer can start refining his search in the new market for a site that has these characteristics. Of course, there are no guarantees—every location and market is different, but with a well-developed profile of the characteristics of a location that has proven to work in one market, the retailer is armed with information to improve the odds of success in a new market.

Existing markets

Opening additional stores in a market where you have existing stores is a trickier business. The ultimate objective of opening an additional location is to generate incremental traffic and sales. That said, retailers need to be careful to avoid opening a location that cannibalizes traffic and sales from an existing location—or, at least, they need to ensure that the cannibalization effect is minimized.

Impact on existing stores

Opening another location (or locations) in a market where you have an existing location is exciting and nerve-racking. If you place the new store in a great location, you will increase your profile within the market and capture incremental sales—and you'll be able to serve customers better. Growth is fun! That said, if, at the end of the day, your new location simply shifts traffic and sales from an existing location to your new location, are you really ahead? Probably not. You have just sunk a bunch of money into building or renovating the new location, hired more staff, bought more inventory, and significantly increased the complexity of managing your business for a lot less than you were expecting in additional sales revenue.

Although it is impossible to predict exactly what impact a new location will have on existing locations, understanding traffic patterns and volume levels at the existing sites can certainly help you make a better location decision. Naturally, you will also need to consider all the many factors that go into a good location decision, like competitor locations, the location of complimentary businesses, zoning restrictions, lease and land costs, general accessibility, and more. The point is, location decisions are big bets and there are many, many factors that need to be considered.

Although all the gory details of location strategy are better left to location gurus, the following example will show you how you can use traffic information as a important input into location decisions.

Tamiko Furniture: A case study in location analysis

Tamiko Furniture is a successful, retail chain located in San Francisco. Tamiko specializes in fashionable, mid-market furniture from Japan. With the popularity of Feng Shui, Tamiko Matsuda's furniture has become very popular. During her 7 years since opening her first store, Tamiko now has three locations throughout the Bay area. Although Tamiko is pleased with her growth, she feels she could reach even more customers (and existing ones better) with a fourth location.

The chart in Figure 9-5 shows traffic levels for each current location over the past year. While store #2 and #3 have traffic levels that are very similar, Store #1 has consistently higher traffic volumes. Interestingly, sales revenue from store #1, although higher than #2 and #3, is not significantly higher.

Figure 9-5

Tamiko (because she's already read *Chapter 4* on sales conversion) has noted that conversion rates at Store #1 are lower than the other stores. She believes she's already done every thing she can to maximize conversion in Store #1, and that it's simply "maxed-out". Tamiko, concluded that if she could find a location for her new store somewhere closer to store #1, she could potentially shift some traffic to the new store and capture incremental business as well. Her hope is to not negatively affect stores #2 and #3. After considering all the various options, Tamiko has three choices: A, B or C.

After reviewing her options carefully as shown in Figure 9-6, Tamiko decides that site B would be the best choice to alleviate some traffic pressure from store #1 without having a significant impact on traffic at stores #2 and #3.

Once the new store was up and running, Tamiko anxiously compared the traffic patterns among all her stores. As it turned out, traffic was still very high at store #1— higher than she would have

New store location options

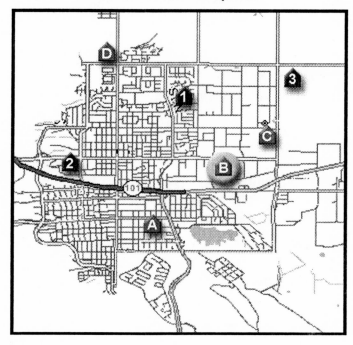

Figure 9-6

liked; however, traffic levels at store #2 and #3 were unaffected. Apparently, the new location was indeed generating incremental

Figure 9-7

traffic as the chart in Figure 9-7 shows. As for the low conversion rates at store #1, unfortunately Tamiko will have to try to solve this in some other way—unless of course she wants to consider store #5!

Corporate reporting

No matter what your corporate structure—sole operator or public-ly-traded corporate colossus, there are stakeholders who will want to, or need to, understand how your business is performing. Even if you're not a publicly-traded company, there are probably a number of outside stakeholders interested in your performance such as private investors, banks, your accountant, *etc.* Obviously, disclosure requirements for publicly-traded corporations are more complex and regulated by various governing bodies. These big retailers are also constantly on the road making presentations to investment banks and other financial "players" in an effort to explain to the market how successful they are and why they will continue to be successful in the future.

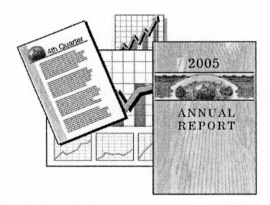

If you spend any time listening to earnings announcements by large retail corporations, you will get a good sense of what they feel is important. What do companies like Target, Pier 1 Imports or Sears talk about? How do the senior executives of these kinds of companies talk about their stores' performance?

The fact is, some retailers talk a lot about traffic volume, traffic trends, and sales conversion rates in detail, while others simply do not. Part of the reason many retailers don't discuss traffic and conversion is that they don't actually monitor traffic, and as we have already learned, without traffic data there is no way to calculate conversion rates.

All retailers talk about sales growth. Often sales are discussed in the context of "comps" or comparable store sales as a measure of overall performance. And this is a good metric to discuss, no question.

The fact is, traffic and conversion are just not discussed enough when retailers are presenting results to stakeholders—period. And they should be. If I was a stock analyst or an investor or a head office executive, I would want to know that management is monitoring traffic trends, that they understand conversion and are focused on driving traffic and conversion.

Increasingly, traffic is a subject of discussion in quarterly earnings results conference calls. These conference calls have become commonplace for publicly-traded companies today. These conference calls usually take place between the senior executives of the company (usually the CEO and Chief Financial Officer) on one end, and a cadre of financial analysts from the many brokerage firms that are covering the company's particular stock. The purpose of the call is to present the current quarter's financial results, provide additional context and perspective on the results, and answer any questions the analysts may have.

Using traffic and sales conversion information as part of the results presentation can be very compelling and useful to management. For the most part, analysts want to understand the underlying drivers behind the revenue and profit performance presented by management. Here's is an example of what one of these conference calls might sound like. In this first case, the sporting goods retailer does not have traffic and conversion data available to help explain the results:

> **Retailer**: "We are pleased with our sales growth in Q3 and are confident that our marketing initiatives in Q4 will help drive sales."
>
> **Analyst**: "Could you describe specifically what it is about your marketing initiatives that make you believe you will be successful?"
>
> **Retailer**: "We spend $40 million on advertising, mostly in

flyers and circulars. When we drop a flyer we know exactly what happens in sales. Although it doesn't always go as you expect—for instance, you feature ski equipment and clothing, and the weather turns unseasonably warm—but for the most part, we know our marketing works."

I find this type of explanation of limited value. What does it mean? Essentially, this retailer is saying "just trust me—I know what works." Frankly, it is very difficult to understand what the performance is, and what the underlying performance drivers are, with this type of information.

Let's look at another example, though this time the retailer uses traffic and sales conversion information to provide additional context to help explain performance and support his strategy:

> **Retailer**: "We are pleased with our sales growth in Q3 and are confident that our marketing initiatives in Q4 will drive traffic into our stores. In fact, we are expecting same store traffic volumes to increase by 10%."

> **Analyst**: "The traffic is good but what are you basing the estimated 10% traffic increase on? And what are you doing to ensure that this traffic turns into higher sales?"

> **Retailer**: "First, we have been testing some new flyer concepts and are pleased with the traffic increases that these new formats have been generating in the test markets. In fact, based on the test results, a 10% traffic increase could be conservative. Second, we have been working really hard on improving our sales conversion rates across the entire chain. In Q3, our sales conversion was up 8% compared to Q2. We have been closely monitoring conversion rates, and have identified a number of locations for additional sales training."

When it comes to corporate reporting, stakeholders want to understand what is driving the performance. Among the many strategic uses of traffic data and analysis, using the information as part of the corporate reporting and communications process can be very effective and compelling.

Competitive analysis and traffic

There are many things we can control in our business—decisions we make, strategies we employ. Pricing, advertising, staffing, product mix—there are a multitude of critical factors we make decisions about and control. Of course, there are also a whole host of factors we don't control, and competition is principal among these. Every retailer faces competition in some way. And, depending on the voracity of the competitive environment, retailers may be heavily influenced by what their competitors are doing. In this section, we will discuss how retailers can use traffic and sales conversion analysis to understand the impact of competition.

Identifying the competition

In order to understand the impact competitors may be having on your business, first you need to identify who the competitors are. Although it may seem like an obvious point—who doesn't know who his competitors are? It is a useful exercise to write them down, both the direct (the obvious ones) and the indirect competitors (the less obvious ones).

- **Direct Competitors**

  These competitors are very easy to pick out, and you probably already know exactly who they are. Direct competitors are the retailers that are in your market space. They have a similar product offering and they are the stores that your customers would also think of when they need to buy something.

- **Indirect Competitors**

  These competitors are less obvious and may be companies that you don't fully view as competitors. These companies may or may not be carrying the same types of products you carry, but either don't offer the products the same way as you do or offer substitutions to what you offer. For example, if you ran a chain of small, neighborhood hardware stores, in addition to all the other small hardware stores in the market that are obviously direct competitors, you would be in competition against the big box hardware mega-stores, as well as other department stores that offer a limited selection of hardware products.

Let's look at an example to demonstrate how traffic data can be used to assess the impact of a new competitor.

Uh-oh, you have a new neighbor: A case study in competitive analysis

Handys Hardware is a smart little retail operation of 7 stores operating in Phoenix. The company has flourished, despite pressure from the big box home improvement chains, in part because the Handys stores are mostly located away from the big retail power centers, and as a result, they have been able to avoid having to go head-to-head with these big retailers. Unfortunately, that's just changed. A brand new power center just opened 3 blocks east of the Handys store in north Phoenix on Camelback Road, and one of the anchor tenants is Build All, a giant home improvement chain.

Naturally, management at Handys is concerned about how this new Build All store will impact sales at the Camelback location. Frankly, they are expecting the worst. Build All has a vast array of home improvement and gardening products—you name it, they have it. And because of their size, they have buying power that is virtually unmatched in the industry. They buy in mass volume and offer products at prices that just can't be beat.

Traffic before and after

The chart in Figure 9-8 shows daily traffic levels at Handys before and after the grand opening of the Build All store. As you can clearly see, the grand opening greatly affected traffic at the Handys store; however, a week later, traffic levels began to rise and four weeks after the grand opening traffic levels had actually increased over historical levels!

How could this be possible? Why hasn't traffic at Handys simply dwindled to virtually nothing? Why hasn't Build All, with their vast product offering and rock bottom prices, annihilated Handys?

In this case, the traffic response to the new competitor is not completely unexpected. Though the grand opening of Build All did negatively impact traffic in the short term, the impact apparently

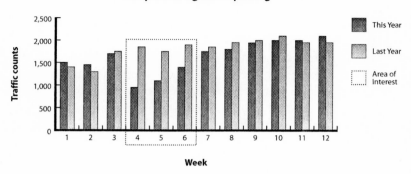

Weekly traffic before and after competitor's grand opening

Figure 9-8

was not sustained. This could be explained by customers sampling the new mega store—naturally customers will be curious and will want to see what the new store is all about. However, there is no guarantee that they will appreciate what they see. In this case, the Build All store is many times larger than the Handys store, which to some customers means that it's a lot harder to find what they're looking for. And as far as pricing is concerned, Build All has great pricing—even a lot better than Handys—but the line-ups at the cash outs and the congestion in the parking lot make it a real hassle to shop there. Lastly, because Build All spends a significant amount on advertising and promotions, they attracted more prospect customers into the entire trading area. Some of these new prospects that might not have visited the area otherwise, came out to Camelback Road, where, because of the close proximity, also saw the Handys store and stopped by.

Using traffic data as a competitive advantage

In the Handys Hardware example, the story has a happy ending—traffic actually went up as a result of a competitor. However, clearly that's not always the case. In fact, the story could have had a very unhappy outcome if, for example, traffic at the Handys store dropped by 50% during the Build All grand opening and then stayed there! This could prove to be fatal, at least for this one location. So as a retailer, how can you use traffic information to help you combat the competition?

Step 1: Measure the traffic impact

As we saw in the Handys example, you won't understand what the impact is unless you measure it. Analyze traffic levels by day, and even by hour, through the grand opening and the subsequent weeks. Look for any changes to the patterns and volumes. Make sure you compare traffic level trends as well as year-over-year comparatives. You need to ensure that you are not just seeing changes in general business seasonality. If traffic has decreased and sustains at lower levels, obviously, management needs to be concerned with traffic and may want to consider investing in traffic stimulation activities, like advertising, to help bring more prospects into the store.

Step 2: Analyze the impact on sales conversion

In addition to traffic, management needs to understand what impact (if any) there was on sales conversion rates. Even though traffic has decreased, if conversion rates have increased (*i.e.* because staff are able to serve the fewer customers that come into the store better), the net financial impact on the retailer may be minimized. If management can't find the money to do expensive traffic stimulation advertising, they need to ensure they make the most of every sales opportunity that comes into the store. Sales conversion rates will be the key measure of whether the retailer is being more efficient and effective in the face of reduced traffic. If traffic and sales conversion rates are dropping, this is a very serious situation for management. In this case, management can continue to monitor the situation—do nothing, in other words. Or, management can devise new strategies to help drive the business—use advertising to drive traffic, improve conversion rates through sales training, increase staffing levels, change product mix in order to differentiate from the competitor, to name a few. The fact is, if traffic and conversion have dropped significantly and appear to be sustaining at a lower level, management needs to do something.

Step 3: Identify areas to exploit, make changes and re-measure

Regardless of what strategies management ultimately decides to pursue, the key is to measure and re-measure. What's happening to traffic? Sales conversion rates? By analyzing traffic and sales conversion, management will know what impact, if any, their strategies are having. If the strategy isn't working, it's back to the drawing board.

Although we can't control the competition, it is vital that we understand what impact the competition is having on our business. Jumping to conclusions about the magnitude of the impact can be debilitating to management—what if Handys just decided they couldn't compete with Build All and packed up the store? In this case, it would have been a bad move, but the point is you need to understand what the impact is, and traffic data will provide management with very specific and quantitative feedback about that impact. When sales conversion is also considered, management will have a very good understanding of what's happening in their business.

There are no easy answers when it comes to dealing with a potentially aggressive competitor, but if retailers don't have traffic and conversion data, they can't truly measure the impact of the competitor, they won't be able to identify what to focus on (traffic, sales conversion, or both), and lastly, they won't be able to see if any changes they've implemented are actually making a difference.

Planning and modeling

Because of the inherently quantitative nature of traffic data, it is extremely useful for all types of planning and financial analysis. If traffic data is available for multiple years, it also can be very useful in forecasting future performance. In this section we will review some of the ways traffic data can be used for budgeting and financial modeling.

Advertising planning

When it's time to prepare the annual marketing plan, many retailers will turn to sales in order to determine the best time to invest in advertising. Notwithstanding the normal retail events that may impact business (*e.g.* Christmas, Back-to-School, *etc.*) using traffic data to determine when to advertise can be more effective than looking at sales data alone. For example, the chart in Figure 9-9 shows traffic volume by month for a retailer. If this retailer compared sales by month, the spike in January, February, and August may or may not be evident. Here's why. In this case, the retailer sells consumer electronic products including personal computers, home theatres, high-end sound systems and other electronic equipment. By and large, the products are expensive and definitely fall into the category of high-involvement purchase. That is, prospects don't typically purchase right away—there may be several visits to the store to discuss the feature products available, the specifics of a customized package, and of course, financing.

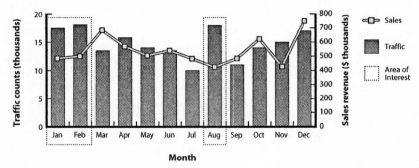

Figure 9-9

In this example, the actual buying cycle typically takes two or three months. Identifying when prospects actually visit the store is a better indicator of buying predisposition and will provide management with an important perspective on when to schedule advertising activities.

Identifying long-term staffing requirements

With an understanding of traffic patterns and how they may be changing over time, management can use traffic data to refine their staffing assumptions, and consequently, use it to help with long-term staff planning. For example, if a large national retail chain had the traffic trend data from each location in the chain, this data could be compiled and aggregated to provide head office with a view of what the store level staffing requirement might be based on the trends. Figure 9-10 illustrates how this information could be rolled-up across the chain. In this example, let's say traffic was up 15% in Territory 1, up 10% in Territory 2, and flat in Territory 3. Based on these trends, head office might forecast a commensurate increase in staff levels for the areas that had the strong traffic growth trends. Although not every employee in a large retail organization is hired as front line, the vast majority of personnel are hired to serve customers, and by knowing how many customers are visiting the stores, management can gain insight into their long-term staffing needs.

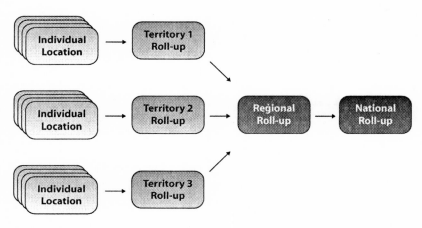

Figure 9-10

Forecasting new market opportunities

Opening a new location or launching a store in a new market represents huge investments and potentially huge risks for retailers. Obviously, retailers are advised to think carefully about the decision, and there are a multitude of analysis techniques they should employ before deciding to proceed. Traffic data can provide some important insights into expected performance in a new location, and can, very quickly after launch, provide critical measures about how the new location is actually performing.

Based on the size and location of the new store, management can estimate what the traffic and sales conversion should be for the new location. Once the store opens, management can immediately look at the traffic and conversion data in order to gage if the store, even in these very early days, is performing as expected.

Benchmarking and performance targets

As discussed in previous chapters, understanding true performance is critical. Specifically, understanding how effective any given store is at converting its traffic into sales is critical. Although each location is unique, and consequently will have slightly different performance imperatives, it makes sense for performance targets to be set across the entire chain by senior management. Let's review some examples of performance targets that could be identified using traffic data.

- **Traffic volume targets**

  In order to focus the marketing department's effort on driving prospects, management could devise traffic volume targets. These targets would set out the level of traffic volume management expects the marketing efforts to generate. Without prospect traffic coming in the store, there is no opportunity for conversion so it is imperative that the marketing investments (or at least a big portion of them) are used to stimulate a traffic response. Traffic targets could help with this. For example, all A stores in the chain are expected to receive a minimum of 30,000 prospects per month during Q3.

- **Sales conversion targets**

  Although there are factors that will influence conversion as discussed in *Chapter 4*, setting general guidelines for sales conversion rates across the chain will focus sales management efforts on ensuring that the targets are met or exceeded. For example, all stores must achieve a 35% average sales conversion rate during August.

- **Staffing guidelines**

  With a sufficient amount of traffic data at their disposal, it would be a relatively straight-forward exercise to create some general staffing level guidelines that could be used by store level managers to guide their day-to-day staffing decisions. For example, based on data from numerous locations, management has identified optimal staffing levels based on traffic levels and have created the following guidelines that managers (especially new managers) are expected to follow. With guidelines like these, managers have some flexibility in decision-making based on the actual traffic in their particular store, and head office has a way to control the process.

Franchise support

Retail organizations that are run entirely as a franchise operation or retail chains that are partly comprised of franchises, present unique opportunities—and challenges! As a franchisee, there is an expectation that the franchisor will provide a store brand or banner, buying power, business processes, marketing support, training, and even more.

Just as in non-franchise retail operations, having data on traffic volumes and sales conversion rates can be extremely useful, and maybe even more so. Here's why. To a large extent, franchisees expect that the franchisor will actively assist the franchisee in being successful—that is the one of the huge advantages that franchises can have over going it yourself, as an independent. However, when the performance and results aren't what the franchisee or franchisor expects, the relationship can become strained. This rarely makes for an effective or constructive environment. Here's just some of the ways traffic data can be used effectively in a franchise operation:

- **Establishing performance measures and indexes**

  As in any other chain, traffic and conversion will vary by location. By creating traffic and conversion indexes, and then sharing this data with franchisees, the franchisor can provide invaluable insight to the franchisees about their performance. Then management can use this information as a basis for working with each franchisee to help them drive performance in their location. The franchisee would likely be very grateful. And, because the data is highly quantitative, conversations about performance become far less awkward.

- **Support marketing investments**

  In a franchise arrangement, franchisees often pay a percentage of revenue into a marketing fund. These marketing funds are used to help promote the network. In some cases, this has been controversial as franchisees pay in but sometimes don't feel like they're getting good value for their marketing dollars. With traffic data, the franchisor could substantiate the effectiveness of the marketing investments by showing the precise traffic response that the advertising is generating. Of course, if the franchisor's advertising isn't working, it's better that they know and take corrective steps rather than having to fight with disgruntled franchisees.

• **Pinpoint performance issues**

Armed with traffic and sales conversion data, the franchisor will be able to understand what the performance imperative is for each franchise location. Is traffic low? Are conversion rates low? Could sales training help? Is staffing too low? Most franchise operations have business experts who are employed to work with the franchisees to support them and help them become successful. Traffic data is a great way to support a franchise operation.

Chapter Summary

- Traffic data and analysis can and should be used for strategic purposes. Often regarded as a tactical tool, traffic analysis provides powerful insights that head office and senior executives need to understand.

- At the highest level, management needs to understand the long-term traffic trends. Long-term traffic patterns are among the most critical metrics in understanding not only the current health, but also the future prospects for a retailer. Looking at revenue trends will not provide a sufficient view of true performance, as increasing average sale values could mask potentially dangerous declines in traffic volumes.

- Traffic analysis can also provide important insights into the impact competitors may be having on your business. Although we can't control what our competitors do, it is critical that retailers understand what the impact a competitor has on traffic and sales conversion. Without closely analyzing this information, it may be impossible to really understand what the impact is—before it's too late, that is.

- Traffic data can also play a role in overall business planning such as advertising scheduling, staff planning, and forecasting. Traffic data can be used as an input for setting benchmarks and targets to be used in driving performance across the entire chain.

- For publicly-traded companies that have specific and rigorous reporting requirements, traffic data can be extremely useful in helping management communicate what the drivers behind the business are, and describe the underlying drivers behind the sales results.

- For franchise operations, traffic data is a powerful tool in helping the franchisor define success, understand performance, and ultimately help the franchisees become more successful.

- Traffic is the fundamental building block in retail sales success. Traffic data and analysis are strategic and it's time that retailers started using it as such. From the part-time store manager to the CEO, traffic analysis is something everyone needs to understand.

CHAPTER

Traffic and Service Businesses

OK, you don't actually sell products *per se*, but your business receives customers—why not use traffic analysis?

Traffic and Service Businesses

So FAR, WE HAVE TALKED a lot about the ways retailers can use traffic analysis to do everything from measure the impact of their advertising to scheduling staff effectively, to monitoring long-term trends. But what if you are not a traditional retailer? To you I extend my deepest apologies. It all applies—every bit of it. To keep things simple I used the term "retail" generically—again, sorry.

If you receive prospects and customers into your location, you can benefit from traffic analysis regardless of whether you sell products or not. There are numerous examples of service organizations that could benefit from traffic analysis including:

SERVICE
BUSINESSES

• Staff planning

• Traffic analysis
  in action

• Why bother
  with traffic

• Banks

• Restaurants

• Government agencies

• Public transit

• Art galleries/museums/zoos

• Sporting events, concerts, lectures

• Amusement parks and arcades

In this chapter we will look at some of the ways traffic analysis can be used in service businesses and organizations. In some ways, service organizations need traffic data for the same reasons traditional retailers need it, but they also have some unique needs that retailers don't.

Traffic applications for service businesses

To state the obvious, service businesses are about service. Whereas traditional product retailers can rely on product sales as one indicator for customer service (*i.e.* if a retailer is doing a great job with customer service, they should expect a positive sales result) in a service business, there may not be sales data *per se* to use as an indicator of customer service. In fact, some service organizations, like government agencies for example, don't really even sell anything; rather, they serve customers, for example, getting a drivers license.

There is no doubt that service organizations have devised various metrics and measures to understand how well they're performing, but like traditional product retailers, traffic analysis can provide additional, important insights that traditional service measures cannot—or at least not as easily. Let's review some of the ways services organizations can use traffic data.

Staff planning

Think about it, by definition, service businesses require some interaction with clients, customers or prospects. That means it is critical to make sure that staff levels map to traffic volume. Unlike traditional product retailers where prospects may be able to wander through the store on their own with no help from staff, service businesses really don't have the same advantage. For example, if you walk into your local bank branch looking to get a money order, you can't just step behind the counter and fill out your own bank draft; self help in a bank could get you 10 to 15 years in a maximum security penitentiary! Of course, automated bank machines (ABMs) and online banking websites have changed the banking experience significantly, but there still are some activities that require a visit to the branch—opening a new account, getting investment advice, getting a money order, clearing up an account error, *etc.* Naturally, as a bank manager concerned about customer service, you would want to match the number of tellers with traffic volumes and patterns—wouldn't you?

Advertising effectiveness

Like traditional product retailers, service businesses also invest a lot of money in advertising. Like traditional retailers, they too need to be clear about what their advertising objective is. In some cases, they might be trying to attract visitors.

If a zoo, art gallery or some other public facility launches an advertising campaign, ostensibly to attract more and potentially new visitors to their attraction, isn't it reasonable for them to expect some change in traffic volume or patterns? I think so. And the methods we use to understand the traffic response in retail stores to measure the impact of advertising and promotions also applies to service businesses and organizations.

Operating hours

If your service organization or business is open to the public, you have operating hours—or store hours. Just like retailers, refining and setting operating hours is a critically important decision. By understanding the timing and volume of visitors in your organization, you will be better able to refine and set operating hours that are best for visitors. Like traditional retailers, operating hours for service organizations do vary by day of week and holidays. How might they change over the seasons? Traffic information could help provide the answers.

Measuring attendance

For any service organization that relies on government funding, establishing accurate visitor counts may be extremely useful. For example, a government sponsored art gallery may be able to support a claim for additional funding by providing accurate visitor counts—if visitor counts are continuing to increase, the art gallery might be in a better position to argue that their site is getting used by the public and that additional funds should be allocated to help support this well-used facility. Here's another one: a university hosts a free lecture by a renowned visiting professor. The lecture will be held in the massive central auditorium. In order to establish the turnout for the lecture, organizers could try counting people in their seats—but this might be impractical if the lights have been dimmed (so that the professor's slide presentation can be seen better). Furthermore, students might come for a while and then leave. Depending on when you took the seat count you might find it difficult to get a precise number. Maybe the next time the renowned professor speaks you can book the smaller assembly hall, instead of the auditorium.

Free admission weekend attracts huge crowds

Journal Staff
EDMONTON

City-operated facilities were flooded by 100,000 visitors over the holiday weekend as Edmontonians enthusiastically took advantage of three days of free access.

The offer was part of the city's 100th-birthday celebration. Fort Edmonton Park and the Valley Zoo attracted almost 68,000 people, while more than

11,400 visited the pyramids at the Muttart Conservatory. The John Janzen Nature Centre drew 5,000 visitors over the weekend and the John Walter Museum enlightened 1,710 people.

Leisure centres, arenas, fitness centres and golf courses lured in another 15,000 people.

The weekend proved so popular, mayoral candidate Stephen Mandel suggested an annual free day be established close to the city's birthday.

Figure 10-1 Reprinted with permission from the Edmonton Journal

Strategic planning

Understanding long-term trends can be extremely useful to service businesses for many of the same reasons it is for traditional product retailers. How are traffic patterns changing over time? Just like traditional retailers, service organizations and institutions operate in an environment of constant change. In order to fully appreciate what's happening and when, you can use traffic analysis to provide invaluable insights.

Table 10-1 summarizes some of the key uses for traffic analysis by service organizations. The list of service organizations nor traffic analysis applications is not meant to be exhaustive; rather, it is meant to provide a sense of some of the different ways traffic analysis can be used by service organizations.

Table 10-1

Traffic applications for select service organizations

Service Organization	Traffic Analysis Application
Banks/ Financial Institutions	• Staff/teller scheduling • Refining operating hours • Location strategies • Advertising/promotion impact
Restaurants	• Forecasting demand • Refining staff levels and schedules • Understanding advertising/promotion impact • Understanding long-term trends
Government Agencies	• Refining staff levels and schedules • Measuring visitation/use
Public Transit	• Refining operating hours • Optimizing routes
Art Galleries/ Museums/Zoos	• Refining staff levels and schedules • Refining operating hours • Understanding advertising/promotion impact • Understanding long-term trends
Sporting Events/ Concerts/Lectures	• Measuring visitation/use
Amusement Parks	• Refining staff levels and schedules • Refining operating hours • Understanding advertising/promotion impact • Understanding long-term trends

Putting traffic analysis to work in a service business

Fitness facility: A case study in improving service

Fitness Land is a very busy gym. They have the latest in fitness equipment, a swimming pool, sauna—you name it. The only problem is that they're a little too successful. According to their monthly "spot" customer service surveys, members are becoming frustrated that they can't get time on particular equipment when they want.

To an extent, that's always a bit of a problem; there are only so many Stairmasters available! Of course, the problem isn't the number of Stairmasters; rather, there aren't enough Stairmasters when people want them. In fact, there are times when you could "fire a cannon" through the gym and not hit a single soul. Management knew that they had to do something or they would continue to see declining customer service, and ultimately, decreases in gym membership renewals. Although management knew that they couldn't buy more equipment to solve the problem, they reasoned that if they informed members about the visitation distribution by day and by hour, members could adjust their workout schedules to come in when there was a little less traffic. The chart in Figure 10-2 shows gym visits by hour of day for a typical weekday.

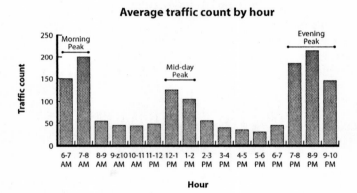

Figure 10-2

By posting the traffic distributions, members were able to see exactly what times were the busiest and plan to visit the gym during off-peak hours. Also, noting the change in traffic patterns over the seasons, hard-core members saw a significant decline during the summer months—just as one might expect to see as people spend more time outdoors to get their exercise. On the other hand, they also realized there was virtually no good hour to come during the month of January when the "New Year's Resolution" crowd came to the gym in droves vowing to shed those extra pounds. Thankfully, the patterns also showed that this traffic decreased significantly by late February—oh well, maybe next year.

"Take a ticket"—why bother with traffic?

Some of you reading this section may wonder with some service businesses, what is the point of traffic analysis? I mean, isn't there already existing data that can tell service businesses what they need to know about the volume and timing of visitors to their locations? For example, if you manage a bank branch, couldn't you simply analyze the transaction details by hour to figure out when you need tellers? If you operate a restaurant, couldn't you simply analyze all the lunch checks to figure out how many people came in? If you ran an art gallery couldn't you simply look at admission ticket sales to determine how many visitors you had and when? The answer is probably—traffic data may well be buried somewhere in the transaction data you currently have, but sifting through it to find actionable insights may not be convenient or practical.

In the case of the bank, it is true that most clients who visit the branch and talk to a teller probably do conduct some type of transaction, but the transaction record may not have been captured. For example, a teller at a bank dealt with three different customers from 10 AM to 11 AM:

1. sold a customer a money draft,

2. assisted a customer in paying a bill, and

3. helped a new customer set up a bank account.

If the branch manager wanted to understand how busy the teller was between 10 AM and 11 AM, she couldn't do it by measuring transactions because there is no one system that captures all of these three distinct transactions.

In the case of the restaurant, it is true that the restaurant manager could sift through the checks to try to identify the number of diners and when they arrived (if they capture timing data). Alternately, some sophisticated POS (point-of-sale) systems actually do capture information about the number of diners and the time, but not all systems have this capability.

So, it is possible to use existing data and processes to get to traffic data, but it can be a pain. And, the more painful collecting and analyzing the data is, the less likely it will be done and used.

Chapter Summary

- Traffic analysis is not just for traditional product retailers. Service organizations can also benefit from understanding the volume and timing of visitors to their locations.

- In some ways, service businesses need traffic analysis even more than traditional retailers because, by definition, service businesses and organizations usually require some type of interaction between personnel and visitors, whereas in traditional retail, prospects may be able to browse on their own or actually make a purchase without the assistance of a salesperson.

- There are a whole host of service businesses and organizations that could put traffic analysis to work, including banks, restaurants, government agencies, public transit authorities, and even public facilities like art galleries, museums, and zoos.

- Of the various uses of traffic analysis for service organizations, staff planning, measuring the impact of advertising and promotions, refining and setting operating hours, measuring attendance, and strategic planning are the most obvious. In some ways, service businesses and organizations need and want traffic data for the same reasons that traditional retailers want it.

- Although service businesses and organizations may have certain advantages over traditional product retailers in that they may already have data that can provide insight into the volume and timing of visits to their location, this information may be impractical to collect and analyze, or be incomplete.

Conclusion
Why Count Customers?

THEY SAY THERE'S NOTHING NEW IN RETAIL—and in some ways they are right. Retailers today are struggling with the same issues they have for decades: staffing, customer service, profitability, inventory management, and more recently, technology.

At the end of the day, retailing is a human experience. Whether you sell cars or clothing or something in between, retailing is largely about people interacting with people in some way, shape or form that results in a merchant selling a product.

Invariably, retailers are trying to get better. Better financial results. Better customer service. Just better.

Retailers are a conservative bunch—they're skeptical, too. I don't blame them. There have been a lot of promises over the years. Certainly, the Web is a classic example of how retailers were sold a bill of goods to, by and large, disappointing results.

Retail, like every other business, needs good, reliable performance measures. Retailers need ways to understand what's really happening in their business.

Many retailers have been operating in the dark. They have relied on history and heuristics to manage the store, and their apparent success and longevity have reinforced this behavior. When there is plenty of money in the till and gross margins are acceptable, "it's working." Whatever "it" is. However, the true test comes when sales just don't show up. As the retailer scrambles to do what they've done in the past (perhaps bigger or faster), and the results still don't materialize, they scratch their collective heads in disbelief and confusion. They look around the room and agree that there must be some big, macro force at work conspiring against them. The retailing gods have not looked upon them favorably—they must have angered the retailing gods somehow. I know, let's sacrifice more advertising dollars—this should placate the angered gods and then all will be well again. If only it were so simple. To these retailers, traffic analysis just seems too simple—how could it possibly make a difference?

If it sounds as though I'm suggesting that traffic analysis is the panacea to all that ails retail, and that by simply looking at prospect traffic coming through the front door somehow retailers' problems will be magically solved, I don't mean to. It won't. It can't. But there is a lot it can do for retailers.

Some retailers agree that traffic analysis can be useful, but they are unsure if they can influence outcomes. This is a curious and confusing position. It's like saying that I know that Doppler radar can detect that a wicked thunderstorm is approaching, but I really can't change the weather, so why bother having radar? I think that any rational person would agree that knowing that a nasty thunderstorm is coming is valuable (even if they can't influence the outcome). Traffic analysis is like that but even better, because retailers *can* influence the outcome—or they should be able to if they're worth their salt.

The fact is, every day retailers are formulating strategies, devising programs, deploying staff, launching advertising campaigns and promotions, all in an effort to influence outcomes—to drive sales performance. They are trying to influence results. But because they don't have complete measures, they are never sure what impact they're having. And they never can if they don't look at traffic.

Traffic analysis is a measure. That's it. It can't fix anything. It can't make good decisions. It can't overcome an aggressive competitor. But it can tell a retailer if what they're doing is making any difference. If it's making a difference—great, keep going. If it's not making any difference, try something else. To some retailers this may not seem like much, but it's huge.

Over these ten chapters we have tried to demonstrate how this old idea of traffic analysis is not only relevant today, but critically important. If you're already tracking traffic, great. Use the information you have—we've just shown you how. If you don't track traffic now, what are you waiting for?

The investment in traffic tracking is modest compared to the benefits it can offer. Try it, we dare you. Because if you do, you too will be able to answer some very important questions. Does your advertising work? What is your sales conversion rate? Which is your best performing location? Are your store hours right? And, if you can answer these questions, you *will* be able to drive performance in your store.

About the Author

Mark Ryski has worked in and around the retail industry for over 18 years. From part-time sales clerk to marketing director for a national chain, he approaches the area of traffic analysis from a retail insider's perspective. In addition to working directly in retail organizations, he spent 8 years with the leading software company Intuit, makers of Quicken® and QuickBooks®, where as Vice President of Sales and Marketing for Canada, he worked closely with some of the leading retailers in North America.

In 1994 he founded HeadCount Corporation—a company that provides traffic analysis services to retailers. His clients run the gamut from small independent merchants to large multi-national chains.

He holds an Honors diploma in Marketing Management from the Northern Alberta Institute of Technology and a Bachelor of Commerce Degree from the University of Alberta, where he also attended the M.B.A program.

Permissions

In order to better illustrate concepts, provide visual cues and, generally, make the book more readable, a number of companies graciously granted permission to reproduce marketing and promotional materials for this book including:

1. Revolve Furnishings, Chapter 1, page 15
   granted by Mr. Jeff Stoner

2. Visions Electronics, Chapter 1, page 17
   granted by Mr. George Finlayson

3. Mobler Furniture, Chapter 1, page 36
   granted by Mr. Eric Fisker

4. Freedom Ford Sales Ltd., Chapter 1, page 26
   granted by Mr. Mark Olesen

5. Hartco Corporation, Chapter 1, page 39
   granted by Mr. Simon Bitton

6. Totem Building Supplies Limited, Chapter 2, page 61
and Chapter 8, page 219
granted by Mr. Trevor Sweet

7. Indigo Books & Music Inc., Chapter 8, page 219
granted by Mr. Grant Packard

8. Pier 1 Imports, Chapter 8, page 220
granted by Kelly Keenum

9. Waterloo Ford Lincoln, Chapter 8, page 221
granted by Mr. Rick Brown

10. Sleep Country Canada, Chapter 8, page 223
granted by Mr. David Friesema

11. Staples Business Depot, Chapter 8, page 227
granted by Mr. Doug Laphen

12. Edmonton Journal, Chapter 10, page 276

Index

A

Advertising
    agencies. *See* Ad agencies
    awareness. *See* Awareness adver-
        tising
    brand. *See* Brand advertising
    budgets 17
    campaign timing 21
    measuring 9, 225
    multiple markets 38
    myths 10
    objectives 11, 20
    planning and modeling 259
    successful campaigns. *See* Success-
        ful ad campaigns
    targeting and segmentation 22
    traffic patterns 23, 29
    traffic response. *See* Traffic re-
        sponse advertising
    unsuccessful campaigns. *See* Un-
        successful campaigns
Ad agencies 21
Awareness advertising 14, 58

B

Back-end loaded traffic 52, 131
Benchmarking 262
Billboards. *See* Outdoor advertising
Brand advertising 13, 14
Brochure ware 219
Buying group size 94, 111

C

Call-to-action 17, 225
Catalog retailing 224
Competition
    competitive advantage 257
    competitive environment 112

competitor analysis 18, 255
direct 255
indirect 255
pressure 48, 256
response 59, 162
Corporate reporting 252
Creative execution 22
Customer
confidence 234
confusion 59
feedback 48
movements 93

D

Dashboard 235
Data reliability 95
Deferrable purchases 75
Destination retail 75
Direct mail 38

E

Electronic traffic counting 92
Executive management 185
Existing markets 248
Extended store hours. *See* Store
hours: extending

F

Flyers 38
Franchise support 263
Freestanding locations 75
Front-end loaded traffic 51, 131

G

Grand openings 163

H

Head office 184
Holidays 158
impact on traffic 159

L

Local chains 180
Locations
city center 76

freestanding locations. *See* Free-
standing locations
mall locations. *See* Mall locations
strategy 248

M

Magazines 33
Mall locations 75
Management
stakeholders 183
Management tactics 79
Manual traffic counts 93
Marketing considerations 17
Media
buying 19
cost 18
direct mail. *See* Direct mail
flyers. *See* Flyers
magazines. *See* Magazines
most effective for traffic 33
newspapers. *See* Newspapers
outdoor advertising. *See* Outdoor
advertising
radio. *See* Radio
reps 20
television. *See* Television
Merchandising 81, 110, 170
Multiple locations
challenges 180
driving performance 195
events 171
performance comparisons 207
performance for large chains 203
performance metrics 187
store hours 60
traffic analysis 182
types of 180

N

Necessities 74
Newspapers 33
New markets 248
Noisy data 102
Non-buyer 104
Non-customer activities 81
Normally-distributed traffic 51, 131

O

Observational surveying 102
Operations management 184
Outdoor advertising 37

P

Performance
    banner versus banner 208
    comparisons. *See* Multiple loca-
        tions: performance for large
        chains
    comparison pitfalls 209
    driving 113. *See also* Multiple
        locations: driving performance
    format versus format 208
    large chains. *See* Multiple loca-
        tions: performance for large
        chains
    market versus market 208
    multiple locations. *See* Multiple
        locations: performance metrics
    store versus store 209
Positioning 14
Precipitation 71
Product knowledge 109
Promotional strategy 111
Property covenants 49

R

Radio 36
Regional chains 181
Regional management 184
Reliable data. *See* Data reliability
Reporting
    corporate. *See* Trends: traffic
Response channel 230
Retailing
    catalog. *See* Catalog retailing
    telephone. *See* Telephone retailing
    Web. *See* Web retailing
Retail sales performance equation 113
Revenue
    traffic. *See* Trends: traffic
Revenue trends. *See* Telephone retail-
        ing

S

Sales conversion
    analysis 231
    calculating rates 91
    drivers 167
    driving performance with.
        See Sales conversion: traffic
        patterns
    factors influencing 108
    granularity 99
    precision 96
    sales staff 109, 169
    targets 262
    telephone 234
    traffic patterns 104
    Web 232
Sales events 165
Sales management 185
Seasonality 26, 49, 77
Service businesses
    advertising effectiveness 271
    measuring attendance 271
    operating hours 271
    staff planning 270
    strategic planning 272
    traffic applications 270
Special events 162
    types of 163
Staffing
    constraints 137
    conversion 136
    estimating counts 98
    expense 59
    guidelines 149, 262
    levels 80, 110, 168, 235
    long-term requirements 260
    measuring performance 145
    sales. *See* Sales conversion: traffic
        patterns
    scheduling 131
    traffic 124
Staff balancing 142
Stores
    banners 182
    formats 181
Store characteristics
    physical location 75

product offering 74
weather 74
Store hours
   competitive pressure 48
   consequences of changing 58
   extending 55
   holidays and special events 49, 170
   hourly traffic patterns 53
   location-specific 61
   multiple locations. *See* Multiple
     locations: store hours
   property covenants. *See* Property
     covenants
   refining 50
   revising 53
   service businesses 271
   setting 48
   standardized 60
Store level management 185
Successful ad campaigns 24

T

Telephone retailing 224
Television 36
Till availability 111
Traffic
   advertising and traffic patterns.
     See Advertising: traffic patterns
   back-end loaded. *See* Back-end
     loaded traffic
   counting methods 92
   dashboard. *See* Telephone retailing
   front-end loaded. *See* Front-end
     loaded traffic
   holidays. *See* Holidays: impact on
     traffic
   monitoring 79
   multiple locations. *See* Holidays:
     impact on traffic
   normally-distributed. *See* Normal-
     ly-distributed traffic
   patterns 50
   refining counts 93
   revenue 246
   sales conversion. *See* Sales conver-
     sion: traffic patterns
   seasonality 77

sources 224
traffic response advertising.
   See Traffic response advertising
trends. *See* Trends: traffic
velocity 126
volume targets 262
weather. *See* Weather: traffic pat-
   terns
Web. *See* Web traffic
Traffic response advertising 13, 16
Training 81, 109
Transactions 89
Transaction counts 95
Travel distance 77
Trends
   long-term 244
   revenue 244
   traffic 245
Triage 167
Turnstiles 92

U

Unsuccessful campaigns 27

V

Velocity. *See* Traffic: velocity

W

Weather
   management tactics. *See* Manage-
     ment tactics
   managing 78
   negative traffic response 72
   positive traffic response 73
   precipitation 71
   seasonality 77
   statistics and modeling 78
   store characteristics. *See* Store
     characteristics: weather
   traffic patterns 70
Web
   retailing 218
   traffic 17, 229
Websites 218
Web store 219

Printed in the United States
25551LVS00002B/226-330

9 781420 824759